OLD TESTAMENT GUIDES

General Editor
R.N. Whybray

JOSHUA

JOSHUA

Adrian H.W. Curtis

Sheffield Academic Press

In loving memory
of my father
Kenneth William Curtis
(1912–1982)

Copyright © 1994, 1998 Sheffield Academic Press

Published by
Sheffield Academic Press Ltd
Mansion House
19 Kingfield Road
Sheffield S11 9AS
England

British Library Cataloguing in Publication Data

A catalogue record for this book is available
from the British Library

ISBN 1-85075-706-2

CONTENTS

ABBREVIATIONS

AB	Anchor Bible
ATANT	Abhandlungen zur Theologie des Alten und Neuen Testaments
ATD	Das Alte Testament Deutsch
BA	*Biblical Archaeologist*
BWANT	Beiträge zur Wissenschaft vom Alten und Neuen Testament
BZAW	Beihefte zur *Zeitschrift für die Alttestamentliche Wissenschaft*
HAT	Handbuch zum Alten Testament
HSM	Harvard Semitic Monographs
JBL	*Journal of Biblical Literature*
JSOT	*Journal for the Study of the Old Testament*
JSOTSup	*Journal for the Study of the Old Testament*, Supplement Series
NCB	New Century Bible
NEB	New English Bible
NICOT	New International Commentary on the Old Testament
NRSV	New Revised Standard Version
OTG	Old Testament Guides
OTL	Old Testament Library
RSV	Revised Standard Version
SBLSCS	Society of Biblical Literature Septuagint and Cognate Studies
SBT	Studies in Biblical Theology
VT	*Vetus Testamentum*
WBC	Word Biblical Commentary
WMANT	Wissenschaftliche Monographien zum Alten und Neuen Testament

Select List of Commentaries

There are several relatively recent commentaries in English on the book of Joshua:

R.G. Boling and G.E. Wright, *Joshua* (AB, 6; Garden City, NY: Doubleday, 1982). The Introduction was largely completed by Wright prior to his death, but the bulk of the work, including the translation, is by Boling. Detailed textual and linguistic notes, and a particular interest in geography and archaeology.

T.C. Butler, *Joshua* (WBC; Waco, TX: Word Books, 1983). Offers a new translation with textual notes and thorough commentary. Written from an evangelical stance, but fully aware of critical scholarship. Very full bibliographies.

J. Gray, *Joshua, Judges and Ruth* (NCB; London: Nelson, 1967). A detailed commentary based on the RSV text. Interested in matters of history, archaeology, topography and philology.

J.A. Soggin, *Joshua* (OTL; London: SCM Press, 1972). English translation from French original; reprints RSV text with some amendments. Balanced treatment of geographical, archaeological, literary and redactional issues.

M.H. Woudstra, *The Book of Joshua* (NICOT; Grand Rapids: Eerdmans, 1981). A very conservative commentary which takes little account of critical scholarship.

Briefer commentaries in English include:

A.G. Auld, *Joshua, Judges and Ruth* (Daily Study Bible; Edinburgh: St Andrew; Philadelphia: Westminster Press, 1984). An excellent little commentary on the RSV text. Although it is in a series intended for the use of the Christian believer, the reader is introduced to the issues which have arisen in scholarly debate.

J.M. Miller and G.M. Tucker, *Joshua* (New Cambridge Bible; Cambridge: Cambridge University Press, 1974). A useful commentary on the NEB text. Particularly helpful on the geographical background.

Foreign-language commentaries include:

F.M. Abel, *Le Livre de Josué* (La Sainte Bible; Paris: Cerf, 2nd edn, 1958 [1950]).

M.A. Beek, *Jozua* (De Prediking van het Oude Testament; Nijkerk: Callenbach, 1981).

M. Görg, *Josua* (Die Neuer Echter Bibel; Würzburg: Echter Verlag, 1991).

H.W. Hertzberg, *Die Bücher Josua, Richter, Ruth* (ATD; Göttingen: Vandenhoeck & Ruprecht, 3rd edn, 1965).

J.H. Kroeze, *Het Boek Jozua* (Commentaar op het Oude Testament; Kampen: Kok, 1968).

M. Noth, *Das Buch Josua* (HAT; Tübingen: Mohr [Paul Siebeck], 2nd edn, 1953 [1938]).

1

INTRODUCTION

Joshua's Place in the Canon

The book of Joshua is the sixth book of the Hebrew Bible. After the Pentateuch, the five books of the Torah which form the first section of the Hebrew canon of Scripture, Joshua stands at the beginning of the second section, the Prophets. The book's very location in the canon already highlights some of the important questions which need to be asked about it. How closely should it be linked with the Pentateuch in general, and the book of Deuteronomy in particular, which precedes it? Should it rather be linked with what follows?

The second section of the Hebrew canon, the Prophets, is subdivided into the Former Prophets (books which have often been described as 'histories': Joshua, Judges, 1 and 2 Samuel, 1 and 2 Kings), and the Latter Prophets (books more readily understood as prophetic: Isaiah, Jeremiah, Ezekiel and the book comprising the twelve 'Minor Prophets'). The question may be asked, then, to what extent the book of Joshua should be regarded as 'history' in the sense of a chronicle of events which actually happened in Israel's past, and to what extent it should be regarded as 'prophecy', in the sense of a proclamation of the divine word to the generation of whoever was responsible for the compilation of the book. An attempt will be made to address these and other questions in the following chapters.

The Authorship of the Book

According to the Talmud it was Joshua himself who wrote the book. But while one or two modern scholars have continued to argue that the book is based substantially on the writings of Joshua himself, or originated shortly after the events it purports to describe (so Kaufmann), such views have been in the main abandoned. There is no suggestion in the book itself, or elsewhere in the Old Testament, that Joshua wrote all or any of the book. It is probably appropriate to think of it as an anonymous work, bearing the name of its 'hero' or protagonist, which reached its final form long after the period in which its stories are set. The question of the individual or group responsible for the compilation of the book of Joshua will be considered in a subsequent section.

The only explicit reference to an earlier source used in the compilation of the book is to the enigmatic book of Jashar (Josh. 10.13; cf. 2 Sam. 1.18; 1 Kgs 8.53 [LXX]). As will be seen, there are good reasons for thinking that other sources were used, notably the traditions of one particular sanctuary (Gilgal), and various boundary and city lists.

The Contents of the Book

The book falls naturally into two major sections and what might be termed a postscript:

Chs. 1–12:   The Conquest of the Land
Chs. 13–21:   The Division of the Land
Chs. 22–24:   The Departure of the Transjordanian Tribes and the Last Days of Joshua

The Text of the Book

On the whole, the Hebrew text of the book of Joshua which has been handed down via the tradition known as the 'Masoretic' is good, and commentators are forced to resort to emendation relatively infrequently. (The Masoretes were

Jewish scholars, active between the fifth and tenth centuries CE in Palestine and in Babylonia, whose concern was the accurate preservation and transmission of the Hebrew Bible. The major contribution of the Masoretes was the development of a system of vowel signs to indicate how the consonantal text was pronounced.)

The translation of Joshua into Greek presents a rather more complicated picture, with a number of different recensions. The Greek recension preserved in the Codex Vaticanus seems to reflect a different Hebrew text from that which is preserved in the Masoretic text. It has been suggested that other Greek recensions may have been edited on the basis of Palestinian Hebrew texts with the result that they follow the Masoretic tradition more closely.

The Greek text of the book of Joshua is rather shorter than that preserved in the Masoretic tradition, which by comparison is fuller and expansionistic. This phenomenon has prompted the question of whether the Greek translators used a text fundamentally equivalent to the Masoretic and abbreviated it somewhat, or whether the Greek is dependent on a shorter Hebrew original (or *Vorlage*).

Some clues to the answer to this question may perhaps be found in the evidence of the Dead Sea Scrolls. Fragments of two copies of the book of Joshua were found in Cave 4 at Qumran (4QJosh^a and 4QJosh^b). The former contains fragments of chs. 6–10, and the latter material from chs. 2–4 and 17. Although these texts themselves have not yet been published, such details as have been made available do allow some tentative conclusions to be drawn. The Qumran fragments tend on the whole to suggest a rather fuller text, of the type preserved in the Masoretic tradition. However, some Qumran readings seem to reflect a shorter or unexpanded text, sometimes in common with the Greek tradition, though in other instances the shorter text is unique to the Qumran material. This suggests that there was indeed a shorter Hebrew *Vorlage* on which the Greek translation depended. It also points to the likelihood that, although 4QJosh is closer to the Masoretic tradition than to that which underlies the Greek translation, the scribes responsible for the Qumran texts of the book of Joshua had access to a source outside the Masoretic tradition.

Further Reading

A very conservative approach to the material in the book of Joshua is given by:
Y. Kaufmann, *The Biblical Account of the Conquest of Palestine* (Jerusalem: Magnes, 1953).

On the text of the book of Joshua see:
L.J. Greenspoon, *Textual Studies in the Book of Joshua* (HSM, 28; Chico, CA: Scholars Press, 1983).
—'The Qumran Fragments of Joshua: Which Puzzle are they Part of and where do they Fit?', in G.J. Brooke and B. Lindars (eds.), *Septuagint, Scrolls and Cognate Writings* (SBLSCS, 33; Atlanta: Scholars Press, 1992), pp. 159-94.

Since the completion of the manuscript of this book, new material has become available in G.J. Brooke with F. García Martínez (eds.), *New Qumran Texts and Studies: Proceedings of the First Meeting of the International Organization for Qumran Studies, Paris 1992* (Studies on the Texts of the Desert of Judah, 15; Leiden: Brill, 1994). This volume contains plates of the 4QJosh[a] fragments, and two relevant papers: A. Rofé, 'The Editing of the Book of Joshua in the Light of 4QJosh[a]' (pp. 73-80), and E. Ulrich, '4QJosh[a] and Joshua's First Altar in the Promised Land' (pp. 89-104).

THE BOOK OF JOSHUA
IN ITS WIDER LITERARY CONTEXT

Links with the Pentateuch

With the advent of the modern critical approach to the Old
Testament, the view became current that it is possible to trace
in the book of Joshua the four main sources which were
believed to underlie the formation of the Pentateuch (J
[Yahwist], E [Elohist], D [Deuteronomist] and P [Priestly]).
Thus it became common to speak of the Hexateuch, that is, a
work containing six books.

This view was not simply based on source criticism. The
events described in the book of Joshua appeared to be the
fulfilment of Yahweh's promises to the patriarchs that their
descendants would possess a land in which to dwell. It was,
therefore, also thought unlikely that the story which unfolds
in the Pentateuch would in fact end with the events described
in the book of Deuteronomy, that is, the acquiring of territory
to the east of the Jordan, and not go on to describe the
conquest of the land to the west. At the same time, certain
affinities were seen between the Pentateuchal sources and
some of the material in Joshua, and apparent discrepancies
within stories were noted similar to those which had led
Pentateuchal critics to propose the combining of divergent
strands of tradition. For example, where were the twelve
stones set up which were taken from the Jordan at the time
when the people of Israel crossed the river? At 'the place

where they camped' (i.e. Gilgal; 4.8)? Or 'in the middle of the Jordan' (4.9)?[1]

Most of the material in chs. 1–12 was thus assigned to J, E or D. It was, however, found to be very difficult to separate the J and E material, and thus reference was simply made to JE. Moreover, the editorial activity of the D writer had on the whole been so thorough that it was scarcely possible to recover the earlier material. The bulk of chs. 13–21 was assigned to P. Of the concluding chapters, 22 was associated with P and 23 with D; 24 tended to be regarded as a Deuteronomic edition of an earlier (E?) tradition.

Although there was some general agreement concerning the delimitations of the sources, the conclusions of scholars who adopted this approach to the material manifested considerable divergence in detail. This, along with the difficulty of separating J from E and JE from D, and with the fact that in chs. 13–21 D appears to provide the framework for P (contrary to the situation found elsewhere in the Pentateuch), has been partly responsible for the abandonment of this approach by most recent scholars.

However, a more compelling reason for the rejection of the view that all the Pentateuchal sources continue into the book of Joshua has already been hinted at. It has been noted that in fact one of the sources, the Deuteronomic, so dominates the first part of the book that it is difficult to differentiate others with any degree of confidence, and that this same source seems to provide the framework of the remainder of the book. It came to be realized that the affinities of the book of Joshua are with Deuteronomy specifically, rather than with the Pentateuch as a whole, and with the books of Judges, Samuel and Kings which follow it.

Although this is a matter beyond the scope of this volume, it is relevant to note that recently some important questions have been asked and suggestions made about the origins of the Pentateuch and about the source-critical approach. A useful survey is given by Whybray, who advances the suggestion that the Pentateuch may have been ultimately the

---

1.   Biblical citations refer to the NRSV unless otherwise indicated.

work of a single historiographer, using a variety of sources as well as his own specially written material. It may have been composed to provide an account of the origins of the world and the origins of Israel, perhaps as a supplement to the literary work, to be discussed shortly, which gave an account of the more recent past.

Deuteronomic Theology and the 'Deuteronomistic History'

The book of Deuteronomy contains some distinctive theological ideas. The heart of its theology can be seen in the opening words of the passage known as the Shema: 'Hear, O Israel: the LORD our God is one LORD; and you shall love the LORD your God with all your heart, and with all your soul, and with all your might' (Deut. 6.4-5 RSV). Despite the difficulty of precisely how v. 4 should be translated (see for example the alternatives given in the footnotes in the RSV and the NRSV), these words stress the 'oneness' of Yahweh, the fact that he is 'our [i.e. Israel's] God', and state that the response to him required from Israel is a love which involves total commitment.

The idea of the 'oneness' of God has a twofold implication. First, he is one in that there is not a variety of local manifestations of him (as was probably the case with Baal), nor is he part of a pantheon of deities; he is unique and incomparable. Secondly, he alone must be worshipped. He is a jealous God, and the worship of other deities cannot be tolerated. The corollary of the above is the requirement not only that sanctuaries and other cultic paraphernalia relating to the worship of other gods must be obliterated from the land, but also that the cult of Yahweh must be concentrated on one sanctuary and others closed down. The worship of Yahweh in a variety of sanctuaries throughout the land posed a threat to his oneness, as well as to the purity of the worship offered, so the centralization of the cult became a key issue (Deut. 12.8-14).

There are several important aspects of the Deuteronomic understanding of the relationship between Yahweh and

Israel. The *land* itself is a divine gift to Israel; the people possess it as an inheritance. The land is the inheritance of *all* Israel, and the unity of Israel is important; it is almost as though it reflects the oneness of God, so that disunity is contrary to the will of Yahweh. Key concepts in the Deuteronomic understanding of the relationship between Yahweh and the *people* Israel are 'election' and 'covenant'. God has chosen Israel and entered into a binding agreement with them. (The making of a covenant can be likened to the establishment of a treaty between two parties.) Israel must respond by choosing to be faithful to Yahweh and by obedience to the obligations of the agreement expressed in the form of laws.

Faithfulness and obedience to the laws are responses to what Yahweh has already done for Israel in rescuing them from bondage and giving them their land. God has shown his love for Israel in these gracious acts, and Israel must respond by loving God. Since loving God involves obedience to the law, it means the maintenance of social justice—loving one's neighbour—and the maintenance of correct worship as a way of expressing gratitude to God.

It is important to note that, because of the setting in which these ideas are placed, there is an air of conditionality about them. They purport to be the words of Moses, addressed to the people of Israel prior to entry into the land. They have not yet inherited the land, and are warned that unless they make the correct choices they will not prosper in the land they are about to enter (Deut. 30.15-20). Obedience and faithfulness will bring their reward, disobedience and apostasy will bring punishment.

It was the German scholar Martin Noth who advanced the theory, now very widely held, that the books of Deuteronomy, Joshua, Judges, 1 and 2 Samuel and 1 and 2 Kings together comprise a single work of immense scope which gives an account of the story of Israel from immediately before the entry into Canaan (Deut. 1.1-8) down to the release from imprisonment in Babylon of King Jehoiachin (2 Kgs 25.27-30). Since some of the ideas which are central to the book of Deuteronomy in particular permeate the whole of this larger work, it has come to be known as the Deuteronomistic History. The last-mentioned event in the work provides an indication of the earliest possible date at which this 'history' was compiled, c. 550 BCE. (Jehoiachin's release is dated in the thirty-seventh year of his exile [2 Kgs 25.27]). It is likely that the work was produced not long after this, during the exile of the people of Judah in Babylon (although some believe that it was written in Palestine), and that it underwent more than one edition before reaching its final form.

The work represents a thoroughgoing attack on syncretism, which had led to the breakdown of religion and society and ultimately to the fall of Judah. It therefore also provides an explanation as to why the disaster had come about. Whether the history was the work primarily of a single writer or of a 'Deuteronomistic School' is not at all clear. The fact that there is an overarching unity to the whole work, and that it is presented in a systematic way, might be an argument for a single person's having been responsible for the compilation. However, there are reasons to believe that the production was protracted and that there were several stages in the process whereby the material reached its present form. It is probably best to think of the 'Deuteronomistic Historian(s)' as redactor(s). Although some material may have been specially composed, much of the work was a compilation of earlier material, probably oral traditions as well as written sources.

This redactional activity involved much more than simply putting the material together. There was significance in what was chosen for inclusion and in the way it was arranged. Indeed, important clues to some of the main concerns of the Deuteronomistic Historian(s) can be seen in the way the material is presented and, in particular, how the material is placed in a framework and sections linked together. The stories of the judges, for example, follow a clear pattern: the people of Israel are disobedient; God raises up an enemy who oppresses them; they cry out to God in their distress; God raises up a deliverer (a 'judge') who delivers them; all is well during the lifetime of the judge; then the cycle begins again. The accounts of the reigns of many of the kings of Israel and Judah are also presented in a rather stylized way. There are

introductory details concerning such things as the king's age
on accession, the length of his reign, his mother's name, a
synchronization with the reign of the king of the other
kingdom, and a concluding summary which concentrates on
the king's success (or, more usually, failure) in closing down
local sanctuaries and concentrating worship on Jerusalem.
Material has clearly been selected because it suits the overall
purpose of the writer; but that it was believed to be a genuine
attempt to report past events is suggested by the fact that, in
the accounts of the lives of the kings, cross-references are
made to other sources which could presumably have been con-
sulted for confirmation, the Book of the Annals of the Kings of
Israel (see for example 1 Kgs 14.19), and the Book of the
Annals of the Kings of Judah (see for example 1 Kgs 14.29).

The book of Joshua, then, is to be seen as an integral part
of the Deuteronomistic History and, as will be noted later, as
making an important contribution to the Deuteronomistic
understanding of what should be the relationship between
God and his people. It quite explicitly links the career of
Joshua to that of Moses (cf. Deut. 31.23; Josh. 1.7), and
presents the conquest traditions as marking the beginning of
the Israelites' occupation of the Promised Land, thereby
providing the context for the ongoing story of Israel. The fact
that canonical recognition was first given to the Pentateuch
may have been one of the factors in causing a separation to
be made between Deuteronomy and Joshua.

Noth argued that Joshua 1 is the Deuteronomistic introduction to the first phase of the occupation of the land, and
that Joshua 23 concludes it, setting out the conditions for its
continued occupation. Within this framework was placed an
account of the conquest of the land which was itself composed
of a number of tales and legends. Noth believed chs. 13–22
and 24 to be post-Deuteronomistic additions, although he
thought they might well have included earlier material.

The details of Noth's views on the Deuteronomistic History
as a whole and on the book of Joshua in particular have
given rise to much debate. For example, not all scholars accept
that chs. 13–22 are a post-Deuteronomistic addition, and it
has been argued that they are essential to the presentation of

Joshua as fulfilling that part of his commission which involved the apportioning of the land. As will be noted later, it has also been argued by Smend that it is possible to discern a number of secondary additions to the Deuteronomistic material; these, in fact, mark a coherent revision of the work which represents a development in thinking.

Further Reading

A.G. Auld, *Joshua, Moses and the Land* (Edinburgh: T. & T. Clark, 1980).

R.E. Clements, *God's Chosen People: A Theological Interpretation of the Book of Deuteronomy* (London: SCM Press, 1968).

—*Deuteronomy* (OTG; Sheffield: JSOT Press, 1989).

A.D.H. Mayes, *The Story of Israel between Settlement and Exile: A Redactional Study of the Deuteronomic History* (London: SCM Press, 1983).

D.J. McCarthy, *Old Testament Covenant: A Survey of Current Opinions* (Oxford: Basil Blackwell, 1972).

S. Mowinckel, *Tetrateuch–Pentateuch–Hexateuch* (BZAW, 90; Berlin: Töpelmann, 1964).

R.D. Nelson, *The Double Redaction of the Deuteronomistic History* (JSOTSup, 18; Sheffield: JSOT Press, 1981).

E.W. Nicholson, *God and his People: Covenant and Theology in the Old Testament* (Oxford: Clarendon Press, 1986).

M. Noth, *The Deuteronomistic History* (JSOTSup, 15; Sheffield: JSOT Press, 2nd edn, 1991 [original German edn 1943]).

M. Ottosson, 'Tradition History, with Emphasis on the Composition of the Book of Joshua', in K. Jeppesen and B. Otzen (eds.), *The Productions of Time: Tradition History in Old Testament Scholarship* (Sheffield: Almond Press, 1984), pp. 81-106.

R. Smend, 'Das Gesetz und die Völker', in H.W. Wolff (ed.), *Probleme biblischer Theologie* (Munich: Chr. Kaiser Verlag, 1971), pp. 494-509.

C. Westermann, *The Promises to the Fathers* (Philadelphia: Fortress Press, 1980).

R.N. Whybray, *The Making of the Pentateuch: A Methodological Study* (JSOTSup, 53; Sheffield: JSOT Press, 1987).

3

THE CONTENTS OF THE
BOOK OF JOSHUA

Joshua 1–12

This section of the book deals with the conquest of the
territory to the west of the Jordan. Chapters 1–5 describe the
preparation for the crossing of the Jordan and the sending of
spies to reconnoitre Jericho, then tell how the people cross the
river dry-shod and set up camp in Gilgal where the men are
circumcised and the Passover is celebrated. Chapters 6–8
recount the story of the battle of Jericho, and of the eventual
success at Ai after an initial reversal. 9.1–10.27 opens with a
statement that all the kings of the land prepared for battle
with Joshua and the Israelites, then relates how the
Gibeonites by a subterfuge persuaded the Israelites to enter
into a treaty, as a result of which Joshua and the Israelites
came to the assistance of the Gibeonites against a coalition of
five kings who were repulsed and captured at Makkedah.

The mention of Makkedah provides a link to the next short
section (10.28-43), which, in an almost annalistic style,
recounts a campaign in the south involving victories over
Makkedah, Libnah, Lachish, the king of Gezer, Eglon,
Hebron and Debir (here a town rather than a king as in 10.3).
It is significant that Jerusalem, whose ruler gathered together
the coalition of five kings mentioned earlier in the chapter, is
not in the list. It has been suggested that vv. 28-39 are set out
according to a traditional itinerary. 11.1-15 describes a
northern campaign in which a Canaanite coalition is defeated

in battle by the waters of Merom, and the city of Hazor is destroyed. There follows a summary of the conquest (11.16–12.24), mentioning the total area taken, the removal of the Anakim (legendary giants reputed to have lived in the land before the Israelites), and the various kings who were defeated both in Transjordan and to the west of the river. The origin of the list of defeated kings is obscure, but it is noteworthy that it includes a number of places not mentioned in chs. 2–11. Some have thought the list to be artificial, but it has also been argued that it is very ancient (by Soggin, for example) or that it reflects the situation at the time of Solomon.

As can be seen from the above outline, the story of the capture of Jericho stands at the heart of chs. 1–12. Chapters 1–5 lead up to this central event, and chs. 7–9 continue to describe the conquest of territory assigned to the tribe of Benjamin. It could therefore be claimed that chs. 1–9 are almost entirely concerned with the conquests of Benjamin. An exception is the description of the building of an altar on Mount Ebal, and an assembly of the people at Shechem (8.30-35), but it is widely believed that this passage is a later insertion. (It is noteworthy that in the LXX these verses are placed after 9.2.) The story recounted in 10.1-15 is also linked with Benjamin through its interest in Gibeon, and can be seen as following naturally from ch. 9. However, it is also closely connected with the story which follows, of the five kings who hid in the cave at Makkedah (10.16-27), and it has been suggested that these were originally one story, now separated by the insertion of v. 15. The presence of the quotation from the book of Jashar may well be significant. It is not impossible that the story of a battle at Gibeon has been produced to provide an explanation for a well-known snippet of poetry, and inserted at an appropriate point in the conquest traditions. It should also be noted that in addition to Gibeon the quotation mentions the valley of Aijalon which is outside the territory of Benjamin. This begins to widen the horizons from Benjamin, as does the mention of Jerusalem and the homes of the rest of the coalition of kings, Hebron, Jarmuth, Lachish and Eglon.

However, although the geographical context is beginning to widen, one thing remains constant for the time being. When Joshua and the Israelites crossed the Jordan they encamped at Gilgal (4.19), and it was therefore presumably from Gilgal that they set out on the campaigns against Jericho and Ai. It was to the camp at Gilgal that the Gibeonites came to meet Joshua (9.6). So Gilgal was the focal point of the campaigns in the territory of Benjamin. But even when the horizons widen, it is from Gilgal that Joshua sets out against the coalition of kings (10.6-9), and to Gilgal that he returns after the initial victory (10.15), and after his campaign in the south (10.43). It is not explicitly stated whence the Israelites set out on the northern campaign described in ch. 11, but the implication is again that it was from Gilgal. Although this lies outside the section of the book under discussion, it is noteworthy that 14.6 presents Joshua as still being in Gilgal, and it is not until 18.1 that there is a geographical shift of focus when the whole congregation of the Israelites is reported to have gathered at Shiloh. (Indeed if, as has been suggested, 'go up' in Judg. 1.1 implies a starting point in the Jordan Valley, it is possible that the events recounted at the beginning of the book of Judges, which the editor has placed 'after the death of Joshua', are also presented as having Gilgal as their starting point. However, the verb 'go up' is often used in a military context to mean 'go to battle' without necessarily referring to the contours of the land.)

The majority of the traditions in chs. 1–12, then, relate to the territory of Benjamin and its sanctuary Gilgal. And even those which apparently have nothing directly to do with Gilgal seem to have been linked to Gilgal by the redactor. Gilgal may have come to prominence with the selection of the Benjaminite Saul as king. One of the traditions about his becoming king describes how Samuel summoned an assembly of the people at Gilgal where sacrifices were offered (1 Sam. 11.14-15). That Gilgal continued to be a prominent sanctuary after the time of Saul, albeit one of which the prophets disapproved, is suggested by a number of disparaging remarks in Amos 4.4; 5.5; Hos. 4.15; 9.15; 12.11. (The precise location of Gilgal is not known, but a small tell about 4 km

north-east of Jericho has been suggested as a likely
candidate.)

It may therefore be surmised that most of the traditions of
Joshua 1–12 originated in Benjamin and were gathered
together at, preserved at and disseminated from the sanctuary at Gilgal. Some, it has been suggested, may even have
been cultic in origin, particularly chs. 3–4, although attempts
to differentiate 'Gilgal' traditions from 'tribe of Benjamin' traditions are, on the whole, inconclusive. Associated with possible cultic features within the tradition may be elements
which reflect the notion of 'Holy War'; the defeat of Jericho
was a divine victory, and the role of the human participants
was to perform what might be termed the appropriate rituals.
The concept of 'Holy War' will be discussed later (Chapter 8).
Suffice it to say here that the extent to which a 'Holy War'
motif was already present in the earliest stages of the development of the traditions, or represents a Deuteronomistic interpretation of the events, is impossible to judge with certainty.
What does seem reasonably clear is that the traditions which
originally referred to a relatively small central area have been
skilfully redacted in such a way as to make them present a
unified account of the conquest of the whole land, although
they do not in fact give any account of the conquest of the
bulk of the central part of the hill country of Ephraim and
Manasseh.

Joshua 13–21

These chapters describe the division of the land among the
various tribes. Lest they be dismissed as rather dull lists of
cities and borders, it should be noted at the outset that they
play a crucial part in the overall purpose of demonstrating
that God's promises to the forefathers, that their descendants
would have a land in which to dwell, have indeed been
fulfilled. They end with an affirmation of that fulfilment:
'Thus the LORD gave to Israel all the land that he swore to
their ancestors that he would give them; and having taken
possession of it they settled there... Not one of all the good
promises that the LORD had made to the house of Israel had

failed; all came to pass' (21.43-45). Thus there is a sense in which these chapters have rightly been described as the heart of the book (Westermann).

In his literary appreciation of Joshua, Gunn warns that something of the 'special texture' of the book is missed if concentration on the action of chs. 1–12 leads to the overlooking of this 'more static, administrative prose' of chs. 13–21. These chapters provide a sense of the multitude of elements that go to make up the people of Israel, and stress the size of the task of giving substance to this entity Israel. They may also imply that occupation of the land involves more than the relatively easy successes described in the earlier chapters.

This section of the book begins with a brief allusion to the territories not yet conquered (13.1-7), then details the inheritance of the two and a half 'Transjordanian' tribes which remained to the east of the Jordan (Reuben, Gad and half of Manasseh; 13.8-33). The opening chapter of this section also includes reference to the fact that Levi received no inheritance of land (vv. 14, 33). (In the book of Joshua Levi is not included in the total of twelve tribes, so 'Joseph' is subdivided into Ephraim and Manasseh.)

Chapters 14–19 detail the allotment of the land of Canaan to the nine and a half 'Cisjordanian' tribes which settle to the west of the Jordan, beginning with Judah and associated southern groups (chs. 14–15), then the Joseph tribes (chs. 16–17) and finally the remainder of the tribes (chs. 18–19). Within this section there are a number of passages, thought by some to have ancient origins, which appear to preserve traditions akin to those found in the opening chapter of the book of Judges and which imply a less unitary conquest and a less complete occupation (15.13-19, cf. Judg. 1.11-15; 15.63, cf. Judg. 1.21; 16.10, cf. Judg. 1.29; 17.11-13, cf. Judg. 1.27-28; and, perhaps with rather less affinity, 19.47, cf. Judg. 1.34-35). Chapter 20 describes the establishment of cities of refuge, and ch. 21 deals with the provision of cities within the tribal allotments in which the Levites might dwell.

The precise origins of the city and boundary lists are far from clear and have been the subject of much scholarly discussion. It is inherently improbable that there would have been carefully delineated territories at the time which the lists purport to describe, even if the maintenance of boundaries was subsequently important (Deut. 19.14; Job 24.2; Prov. 22.28; 23.10). The number of discrepancies and inconsistencies suggests that the origins of the lists were diverse, or that boundaries shifted in the course of time. For example, was Kiriath-jearim in Judah (15.60) or in Benjamin (18.28), and was Eshtaol in Judah (15.33) or Dan (19.41)? Border lists and city lists are not given for all the tribes, and some of those which are provided seem incomplete.

Butler has sought to identify three main types of traditional material within these chapters—narratives, political boundary and city lists, and notes on the Canaanites who remained in the land—and believes that they were used in Israel long before they were incorporated into the Deuteronomistic History. Alt and Noth suggested that the *border* lists may actually go back to a document which set out the boundaries of the tribes in the pre-monarchic period. (Such a view would presuppose that there *was* an organized tribal system prior to the monarchy, a matter which has been disputed and which must be regarded as far from certain.)

Alt believed that the city lists of Judah (15.21-62) and Benjamin (18.21-28) came from the time of Josiah and reflected his reorganization, while others have argued that they may reflect administrative districts from earlier in the monarchic period, for instance the time of David and Solomon, of Rehoboam or of Jehoshaphat. The fact that some of the cities assigned to Benjamin were in territory which usually formed part of the Northern Kingdom may simply reflect the fact that the border was not always in precisely the same place. Although most scholars have supported origins during the monarchy, arguments have been put forward for a much later date. Mowinckel suggested that chs. 13–19 belonged to a Priestly or even later redaction, but Soggin rightly questions whether such lists could have been so significant at a time when there was no hope of a restoration of the land of Israel according to such boundaries.

It is noteworthy that the lists which relate to Judah and

Benjamin seem much more precise than those referring to the northern tribes. Perhaps the former reflect the actuality of some stage of the history of the Southern Kingdom, or, indeed, the Judaean origin of the Deuteronomistic History, whereas the latter are the result of memories of the former Northern Kingdom from some time after its destruction.

Alt and Noth dated the lists in chs. 20 and 21 to the time of Josiah and his plans for restoration, but others have preferred to think of some earlier period in the monarchy, when all the cities were in Israelite control, but after the time of David and Solomon when some of the cities were first occupied. Some believe the list of levitical cities in ch. 21 to be utopian and to lack any historical basis. A similar, but by no means identical, list of levitical cities is preserved in 1 Chronicles 6.

Joshua 22–24

Chapter 22 gives an account of the departure of the Transjordanian tribes to their new homes, and describes how a compromise was reached over the building of an altar by those tribes, to which the Cisjordanian tribes had objected. The last two chapters of the book appear to give two separate accounts of Joshua's farewell address to the people, then record the death and burial of Joshua (24.29-30), and, after a summary verse, the bringing of the bones of Joseph from Egypt for burial in Shechem (24.32) and the death and burial of Aaron's son Eleazar (24.33).

Why are there two versions of Joshua's final discourse? That in ch. 23, which is generally accepted as being Deuteronomistic, is not located geographically, and the chapter's opening words certainly suggest that it is intended as Joshua's farewell: 'A long time afterward, when the LORD had given rest to Israel from all their enemies all around, and Joshua was old and well advanced in years...' (23.1). The address in ch. 24 is set in the rather surprising location of Shechem, outside Joshua's principal sphere of activity; the passage describing the erection of an altar on Mount Ebal (8.30-35) is intrusive and probably a later insertion, as has been noted. There is nothing in this address of a specifically valedictory nature, and, as has frequently been noted, its form appears to reflect a cultic celebration. It has been suggested that the chapter is based on the memory of a 'covenant renewal ceremony' at which the representatives of the tribes would gather together at the central sanctuary to re-pledge their allegiance to Yahweh. (It may be significant that the other Shechem-related passage in ch. 8 also describes a ceremony at which the people pledged themselves to keep the law.)

Such an understanding of ch. 24 tends to presuppose a belief that, prior to the monarchy, there was some sort of tribal confederacy or amphictyony (a term borrowed from the classical world, where it described twelve-member leagues of clans with a central sanctuary, and which was thought to be applicable to the twelve tribes of Israel), and that it was allegiance to Yahweh, expressed in the form of the covenant, which provided the unifying factor for a disparate group of tribes. (It should be noted that the amphictyony theory has largely fallen out of favour, one of the reasons being that there is no real evidence to suggest that Shechem *was* a central sanctuary apart from the two difficult passages in Joshua.) But there has been considerable discussion as to whether ch. 24 is relatively early, or a late post-Deuteronomistic addition, albeit perhaps containing earlier material. However, this type of question introduces the more general issue of how the book of Joshua came to reach its final form.

Further Reading

A. Alt, 'Das System der Stammesgrenzen im Buche Josua', in *Kleine Schriften zur Geschichte des Volkes Israel* (Munich: Beck, 2nd edn, 1959), I, pp. 193-202.

—'The Formation of the Israelite State in Palestine', in *Essays on Old Testament History and Religion* (Oxford: Basil Blackwell, 1966), pp. 173-237.

A.D.H. Mayes, *Israel in the Period of the Judges* (SBT Second Series, 29; London: SCM Press, 1974).

S. Mowinckel, *Zur Frage nach dokumentarischen Quellen in Josua 13–19* (Oslo: Jacob Dybwad, 1946).

M. Noth, *Das System der zwolf Stämme Israels* (BWANT, 4.1; Stuttgart: Kohlhammer, 1930).

4

THE COMPOSITION OF
THE BOOK OF JOSHUA

Traditions, Additions and Editions

The survey of the contents has indicated that a variety of types of material have been incorporated into the present book of Joshua. These include traditions from the sanctuary at Gilgal and the tribe of Benjamin, a couple of Shechemite traditions, some material which may be cultic in origin, and various boundary and city lists. The present shape of the book betrays evidence of its composite nature. This is shown most noticeably in the way the lengthy account of the tribal allotments is inserted. The opening words of ch. 13 appear to pave the way for Joshua's farewell discourse: 'Now Joshua was old and advanced in years...' (13.1a). But the discourse does not follow until ch. 23, where it is introduced with similar words: 'A long time afterward, when the LORD had given rest to Israel from all their enemies all around, and Joshua was old and well advanced in years...' (23.1). The opening words of the latter verse look suspiciously like an editorial attempt to explain the 'delay' (so far as the reader is concerned) in reaching Joshua's farewell.

The presence of two farewell discourses is a further indication that the book has grown through more than one stage of development. This is emphasized by the fact that one of them relates to Shechem, a location which, as has been indicated, lies outside the main geographical sphere of interest of the book, and which, apart from one problematic passage, plays no cultic role in Joshua. It has already been noted that the other passage which relates to Shechem (8.30-35) seems clearly to be out of place. The suggestion that ch. 24 was originally placed where 8.30-35 now stands, then subsequently moved and replaced by a summary, does nothing to remove the awkwardness of these passages. Nor does the view that 8.30-35 should be read immediately following 24.1-28 and that together they formed an appendix. However, it *is* possible that they are to be related somehow to the instruction to set up stones and an altar at Shechem in Deut. 27.1-8, although neither of the possible contexts suggested by the Joshua passages fits the injunction that this is to be done 'on the day you cross over the Jordan into the land that the LORD your God is giving you'.

A further example of evidence of development within the book may be the present position of the account of the allocation of territory to Caleb (14.6-15), since there is another description of an allotment to Caleb in 15.13-19, within the wider context of the distribution of land to Judah. It is possible that the material which now appears in ch. 14 originally stood in ch. 11, where the taking of the region around Hebron and the destruction of the Anakim are described (vv. 21-22), and was subsequently moved to the section of the book describing the division of the land where it was thought to be more appropriate.

The internal evidence of the book, then, suggests that earlier sources have been used to produce an account of an Israelite conquest of Canaan and that some material has been added and some perhaps moved to new positions before the book reached its final shape. That earlier written sources existed is suggested by the reference to the book of Jashar, and it is possible that such traditions as those from the sanctuary at Gilgal were in written form, although there is no direct evidence of this. It seems likely that some of the lists of cities and boundaries would have been taken from administrative records. But some of the material incorporated into the book was probably derived from oral traditions, memories from the past and perhaps even hopes for the future. The

basis for selection of material for inclusion was doubtless the
extent to which it could be utilized by the editors for their
particular purposes rather than its inherent value.

Thus we can conclude that the book of Joshua was not the
product of a single person at a single time. It contains a
variety of types of material and, as has been noted, there are
inconsistencies, duplications, difficulties in presentation, and
perhaps also developments in theological emphasis. Yet
despite all this, the book in its present form clearly represents
an attempt to shape the material into a more or less coherent
whole.

The Deuteronomistic Editors

As has already been noted, it is now widely accepted that the
book of Joshua forms part of a great Deuteronomistic History.
It is therefore likely that the responsibility for putting the
book into its present shape lies with a Deuteronomistic editor
or editors. The question which needs to be raised here is that
of the extent and scope of this activity. (It will be later be
necessary to consider the purpose of the activity so far as the
book of Joshua is concerned.)

It is not impossible, and is perhaps even likely, that much of
chs. 2–11 had already been assembled into something like
their present form before being incorporated into the
Deuteronomistic History. This would probably be true of the
Benjaminite/Gilgal traditions; but whether the non-
Benjaminite elements would have been included at that stage
is less clear. Nor is it easy to determine whether these
relatively local traditions had already begun to be trans-
formed into an account of the conquest of the whole land, or
whether the figure of the non-Benjaminite Joshua had been
superimposed upon the traditions.

Noth believed that it was possible to discern the activity of a
pre-Deuteronomistic 'compiler' (*Sammler*) in a number of
passages which linked together the main episodes of the
conquest (5.1; 6.27; 9.3-4a; 10.2, 5, 40-42; 11.1-2, 16-20). He
dated the work of this compiler to the tenth century BCE.
Mowinckel too suggested that evidence of the work of an

earlier editor could be detected. This he believed to be a J redaction of the conquest traditions, but, as has been mentioned, links between the Pentateuchal sources (apart, of course, from D) and material in the book of Joshua are very difficult to establish. It is interesting to note that both scholars envisage this literary activity as having taken place as early as the tenth century. Although it may in fact be impossible to be so precise, it is probably appropriate to think that the Deuteronomistic editor or editors used an existing collection of traditions which comprised something very similar to chs. 2–11 of the present book in telling the story of the conquest.

One of the principal reasons for believing that the books of Joshua, Judges, Samuel and Kings are to be linked with the book of Deuteronomy and form a Deuteronomistic History is the presence of passages which are reminiscent of the language, style and thought of the book of Deuteronomy. Within the book of Joshua, passages which fall into this category are chs. 1, 12, 21.43–22.6, and 23. The fact that these passages come at key stages of the book will immediately be apparent. Chapter 1 provides an introduction to the stories of conquest; ch. 12 gives a summary of the conquest; 21.43–22.6 is a summary of the allocation of the land; ch. 23 is Joshua's farewell discourse. Much of the material within three of these passages (i.e. excluding ch. 12) takes the form of speeches of encouragement and exhortation to the people. Here, then, is the overall editorial framework of the book.

In considering evidence for the composite nature of the book, it was noted that the details of the allocation of territory to the tribes appear to have been inserted as something of an afterthought, after a statement about Joshua's advancing years which appears to be a preparation for his farewell address. Some have argued that this addition was post-Deuteronomistic, but that this is not the case is suggested by the presence of the typically Deuteronomistic summary passage (21.43–22.6). In fact the organization of the material describing the territorial allocations into its present scheme (first Transjordan, then the major Cisjordanian tribes of Judah, Ephraim and Manasseh, then the remaining areas) is probably the result of Deuteronomistic activity. Auld has argued that an account of the allocation of the land did feature in the main narrative strand of the book of Joshua, to which some small additions were made before the material was reorganized into approximately its present shape, and, subsequently, appendices on the Levitical cities and cities of refuge were added. Does all this imply that the Deuteronomistic editing did not take place at one time, but in stages?

A further problem is created by the second farewell address in ch. 24. As has been mentioned, the passage with which it can be most closely linked is 8.30-35, a section which seems completely out of place in its present location. The origins of ch. 24 are very obscure. It has frequently been suggested that a pre-Deuteronomistic cultic tradition has been reworked, but this is far from clear. What *is* clear is that the chapter in its present form is Deuteronomistic. So, we may ask, at what stage in the book's development were these Shechemite traditions added, and is it likely that a single editor would have produced a version of events which gave two farewell addresses?

It is difficult to avoid the conclusion that there was more than one Deuteronomistic editing of the book. While it is just possible to suppose that a single editor might have produced an account of the conquest and, at the point at which Joshua's farewell was about to be introduced, decided to include details of the allocation of the land before the final discourse, it is less easy to imagine that this editor would have added a second farewell address and inserted a Shechemite tradition into the account of the conquest.

It is relevant to note here that Smend has argued that secondary additions to the Deuteronomistic History in fact represent a carefully planned and consistent editing with the intention of modifying the work's overall message. In Joshua, this is to be observed in particular in 1.7-9a (where the emphasis shifts from encouragement of the people as they prepare to conquer the land to an exhortation to obedience to the law of Moses), in 13.1b-6 (where details of territories which remained outside Israelite possession are inserted in a context which is about to describe the allocation of the whole of the land among the tribes) and in ch. 23 (where there is again mention of the fact that not all the previous inhabitants have been cut off, and the people are urged to obey the law). Smend suggests that to a version of the history which stressed that the whole land had been conquered a second Deuteronomistic editor has added an element of conditionality, stressing that continued success is dependent on obedience to the law.

Although the view that there was a Hexateuch has largely been abandoned, commentators have suggested that there are a number of post-Deuteronomistic additions to the book of Joshua, some of which have been seen as perhaps having links with the Priestly material. But on the whole these are merely glosses and certainly do not represent a thorough re-editing. As a result of the work of the Deuteronomists the book of Joshua had arrived at substantially its present shape.

Further Reading

See the Introductions to the main commentaries, and the works listed for Chapter 2.

5

THE JOSHUA STORIES
AND THEIR SETTING

The Historical Context

Much of what follows in this book will be dealing with various aspects of the question of whether the book of Joshua can be regarded as 'historical' in the sense that it preserves genuine reminiscences of events and actions which actually took place in the period of which the book purports to tell. Without prejudging those issues, it is appropriate to say something about the context in which the stories are apparently set.

The transition from the Late Bronze Age to the Iron Age provides the backdrop. The Late Bronze Age lasted from the middle of the sixteenth century BCE to the end of the thirteenth, and during this period Egyptian control extended far beyond its own borders. The region of Palestine was part of this Egyptian empire. The other major power in the ancient Near East at this time was the Hittite empire, centred on what is now Turkey, and as its sphere of influence spread it began to pose a threat to Egypt. Conflict was bound to ensue. Accordingly Egyptian troops were sent into Syria-Palestine to check the Hittite advances. Hostilities appear to have continued over a number of years with neither side able to win a decisive victory. Ultimately peace was established between the two powers, who agreed to control their respective parts of the area. However, this peace was not to be long-lasting. The fact that thereafter Egyptian and, more particularly, Hittite influence seems to have declined dramatically may have been in part due to significant population movements which were occurring at about this time. Most noteworthy was a folk movement of Indo-Europeans from the north, comprising or including the group or groups known as the 'Sea Peoples', who disrupted life in the Greek and Aegean world, moving, by land as well as by sea, through the coastal land of the eastern Mediterranean causing havoc and leaving destruction in their wake. They even sought to invade Egypt early in the twelfth century, but were repulsed in battles in the Delta region. Some of the 'Sea Peoples', the Philistines, settled in the southern coastal area of Palestine.

According to the biblical presentation, the immediate background to the events portrayed in the book of Joshua was the exodus of the Israelites from Egypt under the leadership of Moses, and the subsequent period of forty years' wandering in the wilderness prior to the entry into the Promised Land. It has long been acknowledged that there is much legendary material in these accounts, and that the suggestion that those involved were all descended from a common ancestor, Jacob, via his twelve sons is over-simplistic. It has also been accepted that the period of forty years is probably to be regarded as a round number, signifying about a generation and perhaps reflecting the tradition that the whole of the generation which escaped from Egypt had to pass away before entry into the land. However, most have accepted that there is at least a kernel of historicity underlying these traditions, and scholarly debate has tended to revolve around two issues: (1) the date of the exodus and (2) the location of certain key places, notably the Reed Sea and Mount Sinai.

With regard to the former issue, it used to be believed that the exodus took place in the fifteenth century BCE. This view was based partly on biblical evidence (for instance the statement that work on the building of Solomon's temple began in the 480th year after the exodus [1 Kgs 6.1]), and partly on external evidence (for instance the supposed references to the Hebrews causing turmoil in the area of Palestine in the Tell el-Amarna Letters dating from the fourteenth century). Subsequently, the tendency was for the fifteenth-century date to be abandoned in favour of the thirteenth. The evidence for the earlier date seemed less convincing: the 480 years of 1 Kgs 6.1 was perhaps a round number signifying twelve generations, and the statements in the Amarna correspondence could not safely be taken as a reference to an Israelite conquest. Positive pointers in favour of a thirteenth-century date came to a large extent from archaeology. Evidence was adduced that the most likely time for Semites to have been employed on royal building projects in the Delta region of Egypt (cf. Exod. 1.8-14) would have been the reigns of Pharaohs Sethos I and Rameses II in the late fourteenth or thirteenth centuries. It was also claimed that a number of cities in southern Palestine had suffered destruction in the late thirteenth century, and this was put down to the activity of the invading Israelites. (The strength of this archaeological evidence for an Israelite conquest will be considered in the next chapter.)

The story of the crossing of the Red Sea has inspired a number of dramatic artistic representations of the event, usually involving frightened Israelites making their way along a narrow path between towering 'cliffs' of water on either side which threaten to engulf them at any moment! Such ideas may persist in popular thought but have long since been abandoned by those attempting to give an accurate picture of what took place. With the realization that the Hebrew term should not be translated *Red* Sea but *Reed* Sea, and that the Red Sea itself has no reeds, it was no longer possible to think of a crossing even of the tip of the Gulf of Suez, let alone the Red Sea proper. Therefore alternative locations were sought, and suggestions included Lake Sirbonis, the area of the Bitter Lakes, a branch of Lake Menzaleh, or some other stretch of water in a marshy, reedy area in the Delta region. Some of these suggestions have included speculation as to what type of natural phenomenon, thought by the biblical writers to be divine intervention, was responsible for making it possible for the water to be crossed.

The traditional location of Mount Sinai is in the southern part of the peninsula which bears its name; the identification of Sinai with Jebel Musa ('Mountain of Moses') goes back at least to the fourth century CE and may be considerably older, but has been challenged as unlikely for a number of reasons. These include the suggestion that the description of the holy mountain in such passages as Exod. 19.16-19 implies that it was a volcano, which Jebel Musa is not. However, it is far from clear that this type of statement should be understood as evidence that Sinai was a volcano. It is more likely that this is theophanic language—an attempt to put into words what it would be like if God appeared on earth, by referring to a whole variety of dread or awe-inspiring phenomena. More significant are biblical statements which suggest that the holy mountain was not in the Sinai peninsula. Particularly noteworthy are these words from the ancient Song of Deborah, where again theophanic language is used:

> LORD, when you went out from Seir,
>> when you marched from the region of Edom,
> The earth trembled, and the heavens poured,
>> the clouds indeed poured water.
> The mountains quaked before the LORD, the One of Sinai,
>> before the LORD, the God of Israel (Judg. 5.4-5; cf. Deut. 33.2;
>> Hab. 3.3).

As has been indicated, it was this type of question that was debated by the historians of ancient Israel; the underlying historicity of the exodus was accepted. The fact that there is probably no evidence for the exodus in Egyptian records was explained by suggesting that the episode would reflect little credit on Egypt, or that, from an Egyptian point of view, the event was too insignificant to be worthy of mention. But what of the possibility that the reason for the silence is that there was no exodus? Some scholars continue to believe that the exodus and wilderness traditions are firmly based in history, but, as will be noted later, there has been an increasing tendency to doubt whether there was any major immigration of a new population into Palestine, let alone a military invasion. Some have suggested that there was a relatively small number of incomers, while others have argued that Israel emerged from elements of the existing population of the land.

A comparison of the treatment of the exodus and wilderness

period in three relatively recent histories of Israel reveals the differences in approach indicated above. J. Bright, in the third edition of his *History of Israel* (1981), regards the Bible's account as 'rooted in historical events', and, while noting uncertainties of date and route, places the exodus in the latter part of the thirteenth century. J.M. Miller and J.H. Hayes, in *A History of Ancient Israel and Judah* (1986), are not prepared to reject out of hand the possibility that the traditions may reflect a genuine memory of a period of slavery in Egypt. However, having considered the problems of reconstructing the earliest period of Israel's history, they decline to attempt this, and prefer to begin with circumstances as they were on the eve of the establishment of the monarchy, taking as their primary source of information the book of Judges. N.P. Lemche, in *Ancient Israel: A New History of Israelite Society* (1988), virtually dismisses the possibility that any historical credence should be given to the biblical traditions, and feels that there is no reason even to attempt to find their context. He does, however, feel that the traditions give expression to Israel's self-understanding as a society in their stress that all Israelites are members of the same family.

Much of this discussion may at first sight appear rather peripheral to the book of Joshua. However, the approach of Miller and Hayes noted above, with its specific mention of the book of Judges, shows that it is in fact very relevant. If there *was* an exodus of a significant population from Egypt, it provides the historical background to the Joshua traditions. Exodus and wilderness wandering, conquest and settlement form a continuum, even if it is necessary to ask questions of detail about the biblical presentation of the latter part of the story just as it was about the former. But if there was no exodus and no significant migration of people from outside Palestine, it becomes necessary to ask who did the conquering and who did the settling described in the book of Joshua, and if indeed they actually happened. And if the historian of ancient Israel is to start with the book of Judges, what is the significance of the book of Joshua which precedes it and to which it is clearly connected?

The Sociological Context

City States

The sociopolitical system which appears to have predominated in the Syria-Palestine area in the Late Bronze Age is often described as that of the 'city-state'. The term can be a dangerous one to use in that it may convey the picture of the much later Greek *polis*. However, it is a convenient way of referring to a relatively small tract of land centred on and dominated by a city. This is, of course, something far removed from the nation state where differences of ethnicity or language might divide one state from another. Those who belonged to a city-state would probably not feel themselves to be essentially different from those who belonged to a neighbouring city-state, and might well change allegiance from one to the other as circumstances dictated.

Although it is possible to attempt a description of such city-states, it must be noted at the outset that information from Palestine itself is limited. The most important evidence comes from sites in Syria—the administrative texts from Ugarit (modern Ras Shamra) dating from about the fourteenth century BCE and the somewhat earlier tablets from Alalakh (seventeenth to fifteenth centuries). Both are considerably to the north of Palestine, but the texts discovered there may enable the reconstruction of a picture of a way of life and local organization which may not have differed greatly from the situation further south. There is some support for this belief from another important group of tablets which have already been mentioned, those from Tell el-Amarna (ancient Akhetaton) in Egypt, dating from the fourteenth century. Although found in Egypt, a number of these tablets are letters written from vassal kings in the Palestine area to their overlord, the Pharaoh, and they therefore provide more direct information about the situation.

These small city-states were in fact petty kingdoms. The king was the most important member of society. He was master of the city and its territory, and negotiated with other rulers on its behalf. In addition to his important diplomatic function, he may have played a prominent role in legal transactions and in military matters as commander-in-chief of the armed forces. He was probably a member of a dynasty, perhaps of some antiquity, and the royal family may well have shared something of the king's prominence. Royal palaces, such as that at Ugarit, were more than elaborate dwelling places for the king and his family. The discovery of archive rooms shows them to have been administrative centres from which the 'civil service' would have operated.

The king would be served by a number of officials and administrators, who, although royal servants, may have had considerable influence, and scribes who would record transactions and correspondence. The palace administration probably oversaw the local craftspeople and artisans, and the merchants who traded in the produce of the city-state. Each city-state probably had a small group of professional soldiers, whose functions may have included guarding the king and the palace and maintaining order. All of the above groups may have enjoyed a relatively high status in the local society, although remaining servants of the king.

Below this stratum of society were those who might be termed the peasantry. It would be the men of this class who would be conscripted into the army in times of war, and they may also have been employed on such things as building projects for the city-state. Predominantly the peasants would have been agricultural labourers. It is not clear whether the king was thought to be the owner of all the lands belonging to the city-state or whether the peasants in any sense owned their land; the former is perhaps more probable. What does seem likely is that the peasants would have been required to hand over the bulk of the produce of the land to the administration, as a form of taxation in return for which they could expect the type of security afforded by being part of the city-state. This might include protection against external enemies and help in times of bad harvests. At other times they would be expected to live off what was left of their produce after taxation.

In this type of society two phenomena might be considered endemic. One is that the existence side by side of a number of small kingdoms would almost inevitably lead to rivalries and attempts to gain advantage by a stronger neighbour over a weaker. This would be particularly likely if no great power were acting as overseer of the peace of the region. It is precisely this type of situation which is envisaged in the Tell el-Amarna letters. At a time when Egyptian control over its Asiatic territories had almost vanished, erstwhile vassals vied with each other to advance their own interests, while those seeking to (or claiming to) remain loyal to the Pharaoh begged for help against rebellious neighbours.

A second feature which might be expected to be endemic to such societies is that those at the lower end of the social scale would resent the impositions placed upon them by those who had more power, in particular the heavy level of taxation which may have left them relatively little of what they produced. Such people would become discontented or disaffected, and either rebel against their masters or seek to withdraw from the system under which they felt themselves to be grievously exploited. As will be noted later, it is in a revolt against or in a withdrawal from the existing city-state system that some scholars see the origins of Israel.

The Habiru
Mention should be made here of groups known as 'Apiru, Hapiru or Habiru (or by the ideogram SA.GAZ). The similarity, particularly of the form 'Habiru', with the Hebrew word *'ibrî*, 'Hebrew', has been the cause of considerable speculation concerning the possibility that the Habiru were indeed the Hebrews. This is of direct relevance to the book of Joshua since, as has already been noted, the Tell el-Amarna letters were once thought to contain a reference to the Israelite conquest of Palestine. This was because there are allusions in the letters to the involvement of the Habiru in the upheavals described; and, if the equation of the Habiru with the Hebrews could be sustained, a valuable pointer to the date and indeed the historicity of the events would have been provided.

It is probably no longer appropriate to think of a simple equation. However, it is still relevant to ask what connection, if any, existed between the Hebrews and the Habiru. Some scholars question whether there is an etymological link between the two terms, although others continue to think that a connection is possible. The temporal and geographical spread of references to the Habiru in extant documents is vast—temporally from perhaps as early as the end of the third millennium BCE until towards the end of the second, geographically from Anatolia in the north to Egypt in the south and from the lands of the Mediterranean coast to Lower Mesopotamia in the east. But perhaps the strongest reason for questioning the equation between the Habiru and the Hebrews is that the Habiru do not seem to have been an *ethnic* group. Rather, the various references to them suggest that they were a stratum of society, though this may be something of a misnomer in that they seem to have stood on the fringes of, or outside, the existing structures of society.

The Habiru seem to have had no citizenship and no roots. Sometimes they seem to have served as mercenaries, or on their own account to have become involved in disturbances; sometimes they seem to have lived peacefully as pastoralists; sometimes they provided labour on large-scale building projects. (References to Habiru being employed on royal building projects in Egypt have also been associated with the biblical traditions of the bondage.) Sometimes they seem to have sold themselves into slavery. Lemche describes the Habiru as 'refugees' or 'freebooters' who in the course of time became virtual 'outlaws', settling in areas outside the control of the city-states.

But if the simple equation of the Habiru with the Hebrews must be rejected, is it possible that some at least of the ancestors of the Hebrews (Israelites) were Habiru? The first injunction in the 'Book of the Covenant' is: 'When you buy a male Hebrew slave, he shall serve six years, but in the seventh he shall go out a free person, without debt' (Exod. 21.2). Many commentators believe that the word 'Hebrew' here does not simply mean Israelite, but refers to a Habiru slave. It has been suggested that in this verse we have an indication of the type of situation which prevailed in Palestine towards the end of the second millennium, but it should also be noted that the problem of dating some of the legal material in the Hebrew Bible is immense. However, the verse does provide a possible pointer to the presence of Habiru in early Israelite society. It may, then, be the case that some of the ancestors of the Israelites belonged to the social class Habiru.

Tribal Society

The biblical narrative, of course, presents the ancestry of the Israelites in strictly genealogical terms. The term 'Hebrew' was popularly derived from the name of Eber, one of the ancestors of Abraham (Gen. 11.14-26). Abraham was father of Isaac and grandfather of Jacob. Jacob was also known as 'Israel' (Gen. 32.28) and was the immediate ancestor of the 'children of Israel' or 'Israelites'. He had twelve sons who were the eponymous ancestors of the twelve tribes which constituted Israel. This presentation is clearly schematic. Most would regard it as not having any real historical basis, but as a way of explaining the origins of the twelve tribes and of suggesting their interrelatedness. Nevertheless, the biblical witness is clear that ancient Israel was a tribal society, and, since there seems no reason to doubt that there *were* tribes in ancient Israel, the question must be asked whether anything can be said about their origins.

If the idea that the members of a tribe were all descended from a common ancestor is abandoned, it becomes necessary to envisage that a variety of individuals or groups somehow merged into this larger type of grouping. It may be presumed that some circumstance or set of circumstances would prompt this, for example the need for common action against some external threat or for cooperation in some economic or agricultural enterprise. It is relevant to mention here that archaeology suggests that towards the end of the second millennium certain technical advances were making it possible for new populations to move into previously uninhabited areas, in particular the hill country. These vital techniques involved the lining of cisterns to enable rainwater to be retained, and the development of terracing to prevent topsoil being washed away down hillsides and to create level areas, making cultivation possible in areas which had formerly been unsuitable. The necessity for collaboration in such projects could have provided the impetus for the formation of larger groupings which eventually led to a tribal society.

Lemche draws attention to a story in the book of Joshua which may provide a clue to the structure of ancient Israelite society. The identity of the person guilty of appropriating spoils from the city of Jericho, thereby violating the sacred ban placed upon it, was discovered by means of the casting of lots:

> So Joshua arose early in the morning, and brought Israel near tribe by tribe, and the tribe of Judah was taken. He brought near the clans of Judah, and the clan of the Zerahites was taken; and he brought near the clan of the Zerahites, family by family, and Zabdi was taken. And he brought near his household one by one, and Achan son of Carmi son of Zabdi son of Zerah, of the tribe of Judah, was taken (7.16-18).

A similar story is told concerning the selection of Saul as king (1 Sam. 10.20-21) except that there is no mention of a division of clan in that instance, and this important difference together with the fact that both stories are part of the Deuteronomistic History (albeit perhaps based on earlier traditions) is a warning against the assumption that either story provides a clear picture of the structure of pre-monarchic society. However, this presentation of a situation in which the individual was a member of a family, which in turn was part of a larger grouping—a clan or lineage—which belonged to a yet larger grouping known as a tribe may be instructive.

It is likely that, below the level of tribe, kinship was an important, though not exclusive, bonding factor, and that even at the level of tribe relationships would be expressed in terms of kinship even if this was not strictly accurate. An individual would, of course, be a member of a relatively small nuclear family, although the extended family, perhaps (in the case of wealthy families) including slaves or servants, and 'clients', might be quite large. As intermarriage occurred between families, so wider groupings of interrelated families arose, known as lineages. It has been suggested that ancient Israel was a 'segmentary lineage society' ('segmentary' in the sense that there was no central authority, power being distributed throughout the segments of society), although significant differences have been noted between true segmentary societies and the way the biblical narrative presents pre-monarchic Israel (so Rogerson).

It is much easier to indicate what a tribe was probably *not* than to say what it was! As has been indicated, it was probably not a group of people all descended from a common eponymous ancestor. It is possible that there was a geographical factor, but it is not always clear whether a piece of territory was so named because of the tribe which inhabited it or whether the tribe derived its name from the area in which it dwelt. The book of Joshua, of course, suggests that the pre-existent tribes were allotted particular tracts of land in which to dwell, but, as is noted elsewhere, it is unlikely that this represents the actual course of events. It is possible, however, that the formation of tribes did have much to do with groups, living alongside others in the same region, making common cause to gain a livelihood in the area and protecting it from marauders.

Although this is to move well beyond the scope of the book of Joshua, it is appropriate to note by way of a postscript that it is increasingly being realized that the transition from tribal society to monarchy may not have been such a dramatic and revolutionary change as was previously thought, not least because of the biblical presentation of the events. Rather, the transition from tribalism via chiefdom to monarchy should be seen as a continuum, with monarchy not some alien institution imported from outside.

Further Reading

Alt, 'The Formation of the Israelite State in Palestine'.

J. Bright, *A History of Israel* (OTL; London: SCM Press, 3rd edn, 1981).

R.B. Coote and K.W. Whitelam, *The Emergence of Early Israel in Historical Perspective* (The Social World of Biblical Antiquity, 5; Sheffield: Almond Press, 1987).

F.S. Frick, 'Ecology, Agriculture and Patterns of Settlement', in R.E. Clements (ed.), *The World of Ancient Israel: Sociological, Anthropological and Political Perspectives* (Cambridge: Cambridge University Press, 1989), pp. 67-93.

D.C. Hopkins, *The Highlands of Canaan: Agricultural Life in the Early Iron Age* (The Social World of Biblical Antiquity, 3; Sheffield: Almond Press, 1985).

N.P. Lemche, *Ancient Israel: A New History of Israelite Society* (Biblical Seminar, 5; Sheffield: JSOT Press, 1988).

J.D. Martin, 'Israel as a Tribal Society', in Clements (ed.), *The World of Ancient Israel*, pp. 95-117.

J.M. Miller and J.H. Hayes, *A History of Ancient Israel and Judah* (London: SCM Press, 1986).

J.W. Rogerson, 'Anthropology and the Old Testament', in Clements (ed.), *The World of Ancient Israel*, pp. 17-37.

—'Was Early Israel a Segmentary Society?', *JSOT* 36 (1986), pp. 17-26.

6

THE JOSHUA STORIES
AND ARCHAEOLOGY

Archaeology and the History of Israel

For over a century, the study of archaeological remains from
Palestine and the surrounding areas has made a significant
impact on the study of the Bible. The use of the term 'biblical
archaeology' has been criticized because it might seem to
imply, wrongly, that there is something distinctive about this
branch of archaeology when compared with others. However,
the term does provide a convenient shorthand way of
referring to archaeological discoveries which may be relevant
to the study of the Bible. Exaggerated claims have been made
for some such discoveries, such as that archaeology 'proves'
that a particular event did or did not occur, or that it
'confirms' a biblical statement. Sometimes these claims are
made by those with particular axes to grind about the nature
of the biblical material, wanting to demonstrate that it is 'true'
(usually in the rather limited sense of 'historically accurate')
or seeking to undermine its claim (or, perhaps better, claims
made on its behalf) to authority.

It is perhaps because archaeology appears to be a more
'scientific' discipline—when compared with other areas of
biblical studies such as textual or literary criticism, exegesis or
hermeneutics which involve so much hypothesis and
interpretation—that words like 'prove' or 'confirm' are used
about its results. In fact, there is frequently a good deal of

hypothesis and interpretation involved in the attempt to understand the significance of an archaeological discovery. For example, archaeology may be able to demonstrate that a city was destroyed, but it can rarely prove by whom the destruction was carried out or indeed whether it was a result of natural causes. It has been suggested that the fall of Jericho, for example, was the result of an earthquake. Archaeology cannot prove or disprove this any more than it can prove or disprove the further suggestion that it was this same earthquake which caused the waters of the Jordan to stop flowing. Archaeology might be able to provide evidence as to whether the city of Jericho existed at the time the fall purports to have taken place, and whether there *was* a destruction at about that time, but it is virtually impossible that it could show that the destruction was carried out by Joshua and the Israelites.

With regard to textual discoveries, there seems to be a tendency on the part of some scholars to believe that an ancient text is inherently more likely to be reliable as a witness to past events than the biblical record. Of course it *may* be so, but it is not *necessarily* so. The Stele of Merneptah, dating from c. 1230 BCE, states that Pharaoh Merneptah campaigned in Palestine and won a number of victories, and claims *inter alia* that 'Israel is laid waste'. The word 'Israel' is preceded here by a hieroglyphic sign (known as a 'determinative') which usually indicates that what follows is the name of a people. To say that this stele contains the earliest known non-biblical reference to a people called Israel, and that some entity known as 'Israel' must have existed at the time of Merneptah, is one thing (and this fact is not irrelevant to the study of the book of Joshua). It is quite another thing to be sure of precisely what was meant by 'Israel' and what the significance is of the use of the indication that it was a 'people' rather than a location. And it is yet another thing to maintain, simply on the strength of the evidence of the stele, that Merneptah *did* actually campaign in Palestine and lay waste to Israel. It is not unknown for ancient monarchs to make grandiose claims or to embellish records of their achievements. The fact that the stele says that it happened does not prove that it did happen, any more than the fact that the Bible does not mention it proves that it did not happen. Very few such texts are 'primary' sources, in the sense that they were produced in the course of the events they describe or to which they relate. The so-called Lachish Letters, messages inscribed on potsherds discovered in the ruined gatehouse at Lachish dating from the time of the fall of the kingdom of Judah to the Babylonians, can be cited as an example of a primary source. Most texts were produced afterwards for the benefit of subsequent generations, to provide an account of what was thought (or claimed) to have happened. In this sense, of course, the Bible is a 'secondary' source.

There are many instances in the story of biblical archaeology of scholars' reaching (and sometimes, it has to be said, jumping to) conclusions which further investigation suggests to have been incorrect. Sometimes such conclusions were reached by using and interpreting the best evidence available to the time. But sometimes an apparent desire to correlate an archaeological discovery with some particular biblical statement or episode may have led to an injudicious conclusion. The parade example of an 'identification' which had to be abandoned was the apparent discovery of 'Solomon's Stables' at Megiddo; subsequent study showed them to be certainly not Solomon's and in all probability not stables! Garstang's claim to have unearthed the walls of Jericho destroyed in what was then thought to be the time of Joshua (i.e. the fifteenth century BCE) can be mentioned as a further example.

Problems in understanding and interpreting archaeological data are many and various. The extent to which a text can be understood will depend in part on its state of preservation and in part on how well the language in which it was written is known. The function of some artefacts is clearer than that of others. The dating of an object may depend on the context in which it was discovered. Many ancient sites which have been the subject of archaeological excavations (including a number mentioned in the book of Joshua) take the form of a tell, that is, a mound, usually trapezoid in shape, built up artificially as a result of several successive occupations on the same site. Where this has happened, the logic is that an object or a structure unearthed relatively near the surface of a mound should be more recent than something discovered nearer to bedrock. The aim of the excavator will be to seek to identify the various levels (or strata), and to produce a careful stratigraphy which will enable a relative chronology to be established. Sometimes techniques such as radio-carbon dating will be used to attempt to arrive at an absolute date for a particular level. Sometimes, but only too rarely, an object will be found in a stratum which can provide a pointer to dating; for example, a text or inscription naming a figure whose date is known shows that the level cannot be earlier than the time of that person. The 'science' of dating pottery has become very advanced, so that the discovery of a potsherd or two may provide a valuable pointer to date. Of course, not every tell has been built up in such a neat fashion. The strata may have been disrupted over the course of time, for example by the levelling of a site prior to rebuilding, or by the digging of deep trenches so that the foundations of earlier large buildings can be laid on bedrock. Even something as common-place as the digging of a grave may have disturbed the stratigraphic picture.

It must also be noted that the identification of an ancient site is often uncertain. Sometimes the modern name or the name of a nearby modern settlement will provide a clue, although it must be borne in mind that it has been Israeli policy to Hebraize or to revert to biblical place names where this is thought possible (for example biblical Shechem, which was subsequently known by the Greek name Neapolis and then by the Arabic form Nablus, is again being called Shechem). Very occasionally something found on the site will give the name. Sometimes there will be a long-standing tradition, particularly where a place has continued to be occupied over the centuries. But where a site has lain unoccupied for many centuries and if there are no other clues, it may be necessary to make cautious use of such biblical material as that which we find in Joshua 13–21, which provides an indication that some towns were in close proximity to others, in order to suggest possible identifications. Relatively few identifications can be regarded as absolutely certain.

In the light of all this, how is the person whose aim is to reconstruct a period of ancient history to make use of archaeology in the task? An obvious answer is 'with great caution'. Gone are the days when it was felt that the primary contribution archaeology could make was to fill out the details of a known series of events. Rather, it has increasingly been suggested that archaeology's most helpful role is likely to be the provision of valuable background and contextual information. However, it is important to be aware of the danger of circular argumentation even when making this apparently moderate sort of claim. 'Background' to what? 'Context' of what? If archaeology is used as a tool in the reconstruction of history it cannot then be argued that that same archaeology lends support to the accuracy of the historical reconstruction. What is more likely is that archaeology may provide a context in which certain types of event *might* have happened, or perhaps suggest that it is unlikely that a particular event occurred (for instance if there is no evidence that a city existed at a time when a text suggests that it was destroyed). Attention has increasingly been paid to archaeology's role in providing evidence of such things as settlement patterns, methods of ensuring a water supply and developments in agricultural techniques, such as terracing, which enabled new areas to be occupied and farmed productively. It is precisely to such aspects of archaeology that some believe the historian of Israel should turn, rather than to the biblical texts which are of little value in providing information about actual events in Israel's past. It has been argued that concentration on written sources preserves a misguided view of history; that is, that it is a chronicling of the activities of the great and powerful in society, and that such an approach should be abandoned in favour of one which is based on the trends and longer-term perspectives which archaeology can offer. Such a view, if taken to its extreme, would remove the book of Joshua from the sphere of the reconstruction of a sequence of events which made up Israel's early history.

What is clear is that the historian, if not put off by the apparent impossibility of the task, will need to evaluate carefully the relative merits of the various types of material available, which will include both literary and artefactual material, but will not expect from either archaeology or the biblical text that which it cannot provide.

The 'Conquest' Traditions and Archaeology

Probably the best-known story from the book of Joshua is that of the destruction of the city of Jericho. Excavations carried out on the site showed it to have been occupied from a very early period indeed, with massive defences dating from as early as the Neolithic period, and seemed at first (as has already been mentioned) to suggest that the city underwent a destruction towards the end of the fifteenth century. This was linked with the activity of Joshua and Israelites, and appeared to tally with the statement in 1 Kgs 6.1 that the exodus took place 480 years before the construction of Solomon's temple. However, subsequent excavations at Jericho showed that this destruction had happened centuries earlier, and that there was little remaining evidence from the Late Bronze Age. Archaeology could neither confirm nor deny the historicity of the traditions.

According to the biblical narrative, the Israelites then turned their attention to Ai. Ancient Ai is thought to be modern Et Tell, but excavations have suggested that the site was not occupied from about 2200 BCE until the Iron Age. If the site has been correctly identified, the implication is that it could not have fallen at the hands of the Israelites in the late thirteenth or early twelfth century, as would be required if the exodus were a historical event which took place in the thirteenth century. It has been suggested that the biblical tradition may reflect a confusion between Ai and the nearby Bethel (usually identified with modern Beitin) where there is evidence of destruction in the thirteenth century. However, another possible explanation is suggested by the statement, 'So Joshua burned Ai, and made it for ever a heap of ruins, as it is to this day' (8.28). The name 'Ai' probably means 'ruin', a sense preserved in the modern name of the site, Et Tell, since the word 'tell' refers to an artificial mound resulting from successive occupations and destructions on a site. Perhaps the story explains how Ai came to be so called. (The significance of such stories, and such phrases as 'as it is to this day', will be discussed below.)

It is not stated that Gibeon was destroyed, though that may be the implication. The Gibeonites deceived Joshua and the Israelites into entering into a treaty with them. This treaty led to a coalition of kings coming against Gibeon, but thanks to Joshua and the Israelites, and not a little divine intervention, the threat was averted:

> And as they fled before Israel, while they were going down the slope of Beth-horon, the LORD threw down huge stones from heaven on them as far as Azekah, and they died; there were more who died because of the hailstones than the Israelites killed with the sword (10.11).

The story has become attached to a reference to Gibeon in the book of Jashar:

> 'Sun, stand still at Gibeon,
>   and Moon, in the valley of Aijalon.'
> And the sun stood still, and the moon stopped,
>   until the nation took vengeance on their enemies (10.12b-13a).

Recent excavations at Gibeon (modern El-Jib) have shown that the site was occupied in the Early and Middle Bronze Ages but have failed to unearth any significant remains of the Late Bronze Age other than pottery, which has only been found in tombs. It was early in the Iron Age that a massive wall was built and a pool cut to provide a protected water supply.

Considerably to the north of the area in which Jericho, Ai and Gibeon are located lies the site of Hazor. As a tell it exhibits the unusual feature of a large lower tell which stretches to the north of the highest part of the mound. It was once suggested that this lower tell was a chariot park! Excavations led by Y. Yadin in the 1950s soon showed that the lower tell was in fact part of a huge city which covered the whole area of the mound during the part of the site's period of occupation, and which eminently deserved the description given by the biblical writer: 'Before that time Hazor was the head of all those kingdoms' (11.10b). Evidence was found to suggest a violent destruction in the latter half of the thirteenth century BCE, which Yadin attributed to the activity of Joshua and the Israelites. But how it is possible to be certain that the fall of the city was at the hands of the Israelites is far from clear.

The four sites mentioned so far are, of course, those which figure most prominently in the first half of the book of Joshua—the part which presents the picture of what has come to be known as the 'Conquest'. But what emerges from these sites is that Jericho was probably no more than a hill-fort, if that, at the time of Joshua, that Ai was a heap of ruins at the time, that Gibeon may not have been occupied, and that Hazor was destroyed although it is not possible to be sure by whom.

Sandwiched between the story of the battle at Gibeon and that of Hazor there is a passage (10.16-43) which has been described as having annalistic qualities, with highly stereotyped and repetitive vocabulary. It records victories at Makkedah, Libnah, Lachish, Eglon, Hebron and Debir. It used to be confidently asserted that Debir was modern Tell beit Mirsim. However, this identification is now challenged, and an alternative, Khirbet Rabud, is suggested. Rabud lies about 12 km south of Hebron and was the largest site in the hill-country of Judah in the biblical period. The earliest walled city on the site dates from the Late Bronze Age and four strata have been discerned covering the fourteenth and thirteenth centuries BCE. A stratum from the time of the Israelite settlement lay immediately above the last Late Bronze Age stratum. It is claimed that Rabud fits well with biblical statements about Debir, but it must be remembered that this is one of the most significant contributory factors in the proposed identification of the site. There is a danger of a circular argument here and it is safer to say that the identification is likely rather than certain.

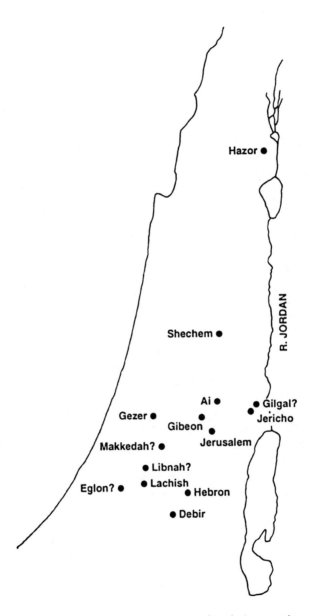

Map 1. *Locations of major sites mentioned in the 'conquest' story.*

The first site excavated in Palestine, by Sir William Flinders
Petrie, was Tell Hesi. It was originally suggested that Tell
Hesi was the site of Lachish, and the published accounts of
the early excavations bear the title 'Lachish'. Subsequently it
was thought that Tell Hesi was the site of Eglon, and so it has
appeared in various Bible atlases, although sometimes with a
question mark. (It is interesting to note that whereas there is
no question mark in the second edition of the *Oxford Bible
Atlas*, there *is* a question mark in the third edition!)

It is in fact all but certain that biblical Lachish is to be
located at modern Tell ed-Duweir. It is possible to speak with
such certainty because of the discovery in the ruins of
Sennacherib's palace at Nineveh of a series of reliefs depicting
the siege of Lachish in 701 BCE. Details match remarkably
with what the excavators have found on the site, so much so
that it is believed that the reliefs were prepared from sketches
drawn by an eye-witness and that it is possible to estimate
where the artist was positioned when the scene was drawn.
The fact that the reliefs are indeed a depiction of Lachish is
confirmed by the fact that they include an inscription naming
the city.

It used to be stated confidently that Lachish had been
destroyed towards the end of the thirteenth century BCE,
although it was admitted that it was impossible to be sure by
whom. More recent excavations, under the leadership of
David Ussishkin, suggest that the picture is more complex.
Level VII at Lachish *was* destroyed towards the end of the
thirteenth century. Level VI was destroyed by fire, and the
presence of the skeletons of babies suggests a sudden,
complete destruction. An important clue to the date of this
destruction was a cartouche of Rameses III who ruled in
Egypt in the first half of the twelfth century (c. 1187–1152).
The destruction could not have taken place before his reign.
Neither level VII nor level VI seems to have been fortified,
perhaps because the city was under Egyptian control. The
most significant point in this context is that level VI appears
to have been the last Canaanite city. So Canaanite Lachish
was probably *not* destroyed before the mid-twelfth century.
There is no archaeological evidence to suggest by whom it was

destroyed. The two most likely candidates are the Sea Peoples and the Israelites. The former would conflict with biblical evidence. The latter would accord with the biblical evidence, but would make it necessary to conclude that any conquest was a protracted affair, and was not complete by the mid-twelfth century.

The three other cities mentioned in this section of Joshua are Makkedah, Libnah and Hebron. Both Makkedah and Libnah have been identified with modern Tell es-Safi, although Tell es-Safi has also been suggested as the site of biblical Gath. Other suggested locations for Makkedah are Khirbet el-Kheishum or Khirbet Maqdum, and, for Libnah, Tell Bornat. In other words, the identification of these cities is far from certain. The location of Hebron (modern el-Khalil) is as certain as any can be—after all, even the location of Jerusalem has been disputed! But because of continuous occupation on the site, excavation has been limited and the exact location of Israelite Hebron is a matter of dispute.

An examination of the stories which purport to describe an Israelite conquest from an archaeological perspective reveals a complicated picture of uncertain site identification, some destructions at the hands of enemies whose identity is unclear, and sites which may not have been destroyed at all at the relevant period. It can scarcely be claimed that there is clear archaeological evidence for an Israelite conquest of Palestine. Indeed, some of the archaeological evidence seems to point in the opposite direction. Is it therefore necessary to consider the possibility that there was in fact no conquest in the sense in which the term is usually understood?

Further Reading

Y. Aharoni, *The Archaeology of the Land of Israel* (London: SCM Press, 1982).

M. Avi-Yonah and E. Stern (eds.), *The Encyclopedia of Archaeological Excavations in the Holy Land* (4 vols.; London and Oxford: Oxford University Press, 1975, 1976, 1977, 1978).

Bright, *A History of Israel*.

D.V. Edelman (ed.), *The Fabric of History: Text, Artifact and Israel's Past* (JSOTSup, 127; Sheffield: JSOT Press, 1991).

J.M. Miller, *The Old Testament and the Historian* (Philadelphia: Fortress Press, 1976).

P.R.S. Moorey, *A Century of Biblical Archaeology* (Cambridge: Lutterworth, 1991).

THE JOSHUA STORIES
AND SOME
QUESTIONS OF HISTORY

The 'Conquest' Traditions and Other Ways of Understanding the Occupation and Settlement

The picture of a conquest carried out as a strategic military campaign led by a single commander, Joshua, is not the full story even so far as the Bible is concerned. For example, the first chapter of the book of Judges presents a much more piecemeal picture, suggesting that the various tribes acted largely on their own. It refers to some successes in ousting the previous inhabitants, and some failures so far as the Israelites were concerned. The editors of the Deuteronomistic History, perhaps conscious of the discrepancy between the two pictures, have placed the events at the beginning of the book of Judges 'after the death of Joshua' (Judg. 1.1a) even though they are in fact a parallel description of the occupation and Joshua is alive 'again' in Judg. 2.6! (His death is mentioned again in Judg. 2.8.).

But it is not only outside the book of Joshua that there are hints that the conquest was not a unified military conquest of the whole land. As has been noted, Joshua 1–12 does not actually describe a conquest of the whole of the territory even though it seems clear that the editors wish to give that impression; how large parts of Ephraim and Manasseh came under Israelite control is not made clear, but later in the book

Joshua is presented as promising that the house of Joseph
will drive the Canaanites from the hill country despite their
strength and their iron chariots (17.14-18). There are also
references to other areas which were not taken (11.13; 13.1-
13).

In part because of the biblical material, and in part because
of archaeology, the very notion of there having been a
'conquest' has been challenged. It was suggested, notably, by
Alt and Noth, followed by, among others, M. Weippert, that
rather than thinking in terms of a conquest it was preferable
to think of a process of nomadic infiltration in which 'land-
hungry nomads' moved into largely unoccupied areas,
perhaps occasionally engaging in conflict with the established
Canaanite city states. The tension between Israelites and
Canaanites was primarily that between nomads and
agriculturalists.

This view was challenged by a number of scholars who
stressed the importance of archaeology. They argued that,
while there were indeed some problems, there was significant
evidence of destructions of cities in Palestine in the latter half
of the thirteenth century BCE, followed by relatively poor
occupations which were credited to the Israelites. Many sites
were newly occupied at about this time, so it was therefore
appropriate to think in terms of a conquest which was the
result of a planned campaign.

A very different understanding of the events was put
forward by G.E. Mendenhall who, originally in an article
interestingly entitled 'The Hebrew Conquest of Palestine',
argued that there was no 'statistically significant invasion'
and no large-scale driving out of the existing population. In
fact there was no real conquest as such; rather, a small group
of newcomers acted as a catalyst for a sort of 'peasants' revolt'
against the existing network of Canaanite city-states, as those
disaffected by the 'feudal' system were attracted by the new
Yahwism brought by a group who had escaped from Egypt.

Then, apparently building upon the foundations laid by
Mendenhall, N.K. Gottwald elaborated his theory that Israel
was formed from 'marginal and depressed' Canaanites. There
was, then, a fundamental breach in Canaanite society rather

than an invasion or immigration. The society thus formed was a tribal egalitarian society, the result of a conscious retribalization process. Yahwism was the 'symbolic expression of the Israelite socio-economic revolution'.

Gottwald's views have been criticized, not least by Mendenhall, whose ideas he seemed to be taking up, but which, Mendenhall claims, Gottwald has exploited by trying to make them fit in with Marxist sociology. In his response to Gottwald, Mendenhall stresses that the destructions at the end of the Late Bronze Age were nothing to do with Israel specifically, but were part of a widespread phenomenon, and that linguistic history suggests that there was no significant change in population. He continues to place great importance on the role of Yahwism in the formation of Israel, noting that 'socially horizontal covenants' are a feature of early societies, and suggesting that the Yahwistic covenant perhaps succeeded because its purpose was to create a community 'characterized by concern for reciprocity and equity'. (It is noteworthy that both Mendenhall and Gottwald have stressed the significance of adherence to Yahweh as a crucial influence in the formation of the people Israel, and that Mendenhall was one of those who believed that the notion of a covenant between Yahweh and Israel was an early idea. Although beyond the scope of this study, it should be noted that the view that the covenant was an early idea, and that it served an institutional function, has increasingly been challenged; cf. notably the views of L. Perlitt and E.W. Nicholson.)

Another important critique of Gottwald's approach has been offered by Lemche, who goes on to offer his own significant contribution to the discussion. The model he proposes is that of 'evolution'. He suggests that at the end of the Late Bronze Age and in the early Iron Age new tribal societies were emerging in the Near East, and he sees the origins of Israel in the emergence of a number of Palestinian tribes which eventually became unified into the kingdom of Israel. His approach shows some similarity to the 'revolt' model, in that he sees the origins of this tribal society in the dissatisfaction with their lot felt by many under the Canaanite city-state system. However, rather than positing a revolt, Lemche envisages individuals and groups moving away from the city-states to find a new life. This would have involved a geographical movement away from the relatively fertile plains, where the city-states were located, into the hill country where agriculture was much more difficult. It is relevant to note here that D.C. Hopkins's detailed study of agriculture in the highlands of Canaan in the early Iron Age leads him to conclude that it was the necessity to cooperate in the face of the crucial challenges to maintain subsistence agriculture in a hostile environment which resulted in the emergence of Israel. Individuals and small groups could not hope to survive on their own, but were forced into 'larger circles of social relationship'.

It is difficult to say what consensus, if any, has emerged from this debate. It may be that none of the proposed models for understanding the so-called 'conquest and settlement' can provide a complete picture of a complex situation, though it is perhaps true to say that the 'emergence' model has increasingly been gaining in favour. The titles of a number of fairly recent studies point in this direction: *Palestine in Transition: The Emergence of Ancient Israel* (Freedman and Graf, 1983); *The Emergence of Israel in Canaan* (Halpern, 1983); *The Emergence of Early Israel in Historical Perspective* (Coote and Whitelam, 1987). What is clear is that it is no longer possible to speak in simple terms about the Israelite conquest of Canaan.

The 'Conquest' Traditions and Aetiology

In Josh. 4.21 reference is made to the asking of the question, 'What do these stones mean?' This question may provide an important clue to the understanding of the traditions in Joshua 1–12. 'Stones' provide a recurring theme in these chapters. Some of them are the result of the destructions of such cities as Jericho and Ai, but there are others. There are the stones with which Achan was put to death: 'And all Israel stoned him to death; they burned them with fire, cast stones on them, and raised over him a great heap of stones that remains to this day' (7.25b-26a). After the story of the destruction of Ai, in a passage sometimes thought to be out of place, reference is made to the setting up of an altar of unhewn stones on Mount Ebal: 'And there in the presence of the Israelites, Joshua wrote on the stones a copy of the law of Moses, which he had written' (8.32). After the coalition of kings had been repulsed from Gibeon, 'the LORD threw down huge stones from heaven on them' (10.11). Then the five kings who had opposed Joshua and the Israelites fled to a cave at Makkedah: 'Joshua said, "Roll large stones against the mouth of the cave, and set men by it to guard them..."' (10.18). Subsequently the kings were killed and their bodies hung on trees: 'At sunset Joshua commanded, and they took them down from the trees and threw them into the cave where they had hidden themselves; they set large stones against the mouth of the cave which remain to this very day' (10.27).

The context in which the question 'What do these stones mean?' is encountered is the story of the crossing of the River Jordan. After the people have crossed the river, Joshua is told to instruct one man from each tribe to take a stone from the middle of the river where the priests had stood bearing the Ark of the Covenant, and to set it in the place where they were encamped. They are to do this,

> so that this may be a sign among you. When your children ask in time to come, 'What do these stones mean to you?' then you shall tell them that the waters of the Jordan were cut off in front of the ark of the covenant of the LORD. When it crossed over the Jordan, the waters of the Jordan were cut off. So these stones shall be to the Israelites a memorial forever (4.6-8).

A similar statement is made later in the chapter:

> Those twelve stones which they had taken out of the Jordan, Joshua set up in Gilgal, saying to the Israelites, 'When your children ask their parents in time to come, "What do these stones mean?" then you shall let your children know, "Israel crossed over the Jordan here on dry ground..."' (4.20-22).

The question relates specifically to stones set up in Gilgal which were apparently visible at the time of the writing of the traditions, and which purported to act as a memorial to the crossing of the Jordan. Reference was presumably being made to some feature of the sanctuary at Gilgal—perhaps a stone circle, since the name Gilgal may mean 'circle'. It will also have been noted that a number of the other traditions suggest that the stones mentioned in the stories were still present at the time of writing. Now phrases such as 'until this very day' or 'as it is to this day' have often been seen as clues to the presence of an aetiological element within a tradition.

The term 'aetiology' is used to refer to a story which explains the origin of some existing natural phenomenon or custom or practice. Originally the term was primarily used of explanations which belong clearly to the realm of myth, explaining for example why serpents crawl on their bellies (Gen. 3.14), or why people speak different languages (Gen. 11.1-9). Stories which explain why a particular place is a holy place by recalling an appearance or self-manifestation of the deity also belong to this category. For example, the story of Jacob's dream at Bethel and the subsequent setting up of his 'pillow' (Gen. 28.10-22) offers an explanation as to why Bethel was a holy place to the Israelites (v. 16), why it was named Bethel (v. 17: Bethel means 'house of God') and why a particular stone or pillar was a feature of the sanctuary there (vv. 18, 22).

When scholars such as Alt and Noth identified many of the traditions in the first half of the book of Joshua as aetiological, there was a tendency to assume that they could therefore have little if any historical value. This type of approach has been challenged, notably by J. Bright. He feels that what must be considered is whether aetiology was the prime reason for the formation of the tradition, or whether it is possible that an aetiological element has become attached secondarily to a story that contains genuine historical material. Concerning the phrase 'until this day', B.S. Childs has argued that it seldom has a truly aetiological function, but more often represents the writer's attempt to give personal confirmation to the tradition being passed on. It is possible that the stories in the book of Joshua which suggest the existence of groups of standing stones or rock formations still visible at the time of writing are to be seen in this light.

Of course, not all such stories relate to the presence of

stones or other visible phenomena. The account of the setting up of the twelve stones at Gilgal is closely followed by a tradition concerning Joshua's circumcision of the Israelites at a place called Gibeath-haaraloth, 'Hill of the Foreskins' (5.2-9). On the face of things the story is an attempt to account for the name of a particular place, and although it is not impossible that the place owed its name to a tradition about Joshua's activity there, it is perhaps more likely that a pre-Israelite name (possibly referring to the existence of a sanctuary where circumcision was performed—so Boling) is being provided with an Israelite explanation.

But there are other aspects to this story. It has an interest in a particular religious practice in that it stresses the importance of circumcision. More than that, it is aware of two other traditions, namely that those born during the wilderness wanderings were not circumcised (5.5), and that only those who had been circumcised could take part in the celebration of the Passover (Exod. 12.48). It therefore provides an explanation as to how the post-wilderness generation were able to participate in the Passover, and underlines the necessity for the correct procedures to be followed in religious matters, particularly worship.

If at first sight the main etymological interest is in the name Gibeath-haaraloth, it becomes clear at the end of the episode that the primary interest may still be in the name Gilgal. In 5.9 Gilgal is related to the verb *galal*, 'roll away': 'The LORD said to Joshua, "Today I have rolled away from you the disgrace of Egypt." And so that place is called Gilgal to this day.' A complex of traditions has been worked together here, all associated with Gilgal and accounting for its status as an important sanctuary. And even in this part of the tradition it is impossible to escape from stones completely! The LXX of 24.30 adds the information (not in the Masoretic text) that the flint knives with which Joshua circumcised the Israelites at Gilgal were placed in his tomb and that they were there 'until this very day'. Presumably some stones were pointed out as marking Joshua's burial and as being the knives used to circumcise the Israelites.

It is necessary to remember, then, that the presence of an

aetiological element within a story does not necessarily mean that the whole story is aetiological. Indeed, it is perhaps unwise to label a complete story or narrative complex as aetiological, rather than considering whether only particular elements which have been incorporated into a narrative should be so described. Only if a story owed its *origin* to an aetiological purpose does it fully deserve the designation 'aetiological'. This has important implications for our consideration of the relationship between aetiology and historicity, since it has often been assumed that an 'aetiological' story cannot be 'historical' but must have been invented specifically to answer some question about origins. The analysis of an element within a tradition as 'aetiological' can be an important aid to the understanding of the development of that tradition. But it must be remembered that an original aetiological purpose may not have been uppermost in the mind of someone who reused that tradition. An element of tradition which is truly aetiological may have become attached to a tradition which is genuinely historical.

The reason for outlining the difficulties associated with the recognition of an aetiological element in a story is not to attempt to defend the stories' historicity. It is to warn against leaping to unjustified conclusions. The historicity of a story cannot be judged solely on the presence of an aetiological element: this is only one of the criteria to be used. In reaching conclusions about Joshua 1–12, another criterion must be the results of archaeological investigations. The reason for questioning the historicity of the Israelite destruction of Ai may have less to do with the presence of some aetiological elements in the story than with the evidence that Ai was not occupied at the time of Joshua.

Joshua the Man: Did he Exist?

Inevitably this question is intimately bound up with questions of the historicity of the traditions preserved in the book of Joshua. When it was believed that the Israelite conquest of Canaan was carried out as a planned and unified military campaign it was natural to think that some great commander masterminded and directed the successive stages of the action. But if it is necessary to rethink the nature of these events, and to question whether some of the 'conquest' stories are historical, is it not also necessary to ask whether Joshua was an actual historical figure?

It is not only in the book of Joshua that Joshua appears. He figures quite prominently as an assistant to Moses in material other than the Deuteronomistic in the traditions about the wilderness period (cf. for example Exod. 17.8-16; 24.13; 33.11). It is particularly noteworthy that he was one of the spies sent by Moses to reconnoitre the land of Canaan (Num. 13.8, 16— here it is suggested that Moses changed his name from Hoshea to Joshua), that only Joshua and Caleb of the wilderness generation were to be permitted to enter the Promised Land (Num. 14.30, 38; 26.65; 32.12), and that it was Joshua who was commissioned to complete the task begun by Moses of leading the Israelites into the land (Num. 27.18, 22). Within the Pentateuchal traditions, then, he is very much associated with the entry into Canaan. He is also connected with the apportioning of the land for tribal inheritances (Num. 34.17).

Within the Deuteronom(ist)ic material, but outside the book of Joshua, he is mentioned as one of the two of the wilderness generation who were to be allowed to enter the land (Deut. 1.38), he is commissioned as Moses' successor (Deut. 31.7-23) and he is described as 'full of the spirit of wisdom, because Moses had laid his hands on him' (Deut. 34.9a). It is reported that he died at the age of 110 and was buried within his inheritance in the hill country of Ephraim at Timnath-heres (Judg. 2.8-9; cf. Josh. 19.50; 24.29-30 where the name of Joshua's home is given as Timnath-serah, perhaps a deliberate alteration of the name to avoid any possible association with the cult of the sun, since Hebrew *heres* means 'sun').

All this may suggest the possibility that there was indeed a man called Joshua who was active at the time when the Israelites were moving into the land of Canaan. But how far the Pentateuchal traditions about Joshua are genuinely ancient and whether they have been influenced by the

picture of Joshua the hero of the 'conquest' is far from certain.
For example, have traditions which associated Joshua with
the time of Moses, and therefore implicitly with the generation
which did not enter the Promised Land, and traditions which
depicted Joshua as active within the land of Canaan been
reconciled by making Joshua one of only two people who
'unreservedly followed the LORD' (Num. 32.12)? It is noteworthy, given the passages listed above which couple Caleb
and Joshua as those permitted to enter the land, that the pair
are directly linked together in the material in the book of
Numbers, traditionally thought to come from the Priestly
strand and therefore to be relatively late; however, in the first
chapter of Deuteronomy, there is firstly a reference to Caleb
alone (v. 36), followed by a statement that not even Moses will
be allowed to enter (v. 37), and only then is Joshua mentioned
(v. 38). Is this evidence that Joshua was only gradually
accommodated within the traditions?

It is particularly important to recall at this point that the
bulk of the traditions in the first half of the book of Joshua
appear to be Benjaminite. But the biblical traditions seem to
suggest that Joshua was *not* from the tribe of Benjamin, but
an Ephraimite. The book of Joshua itself associates him with
the territory of Ephraim (19.49-50; 24.29-30) and there are
other statements which also indicate this (Num. 13.8, 16; cf.
1 Chron. 7.27). Even if Ephraim, Manasseh and Benjamin
together formed a 'Rachel group', is it likely that an
Ephraimite would have played such a prominent role in the
activities of the Benjaminites as is suggested by chs. 1-12, or
would he have been more at home in a rather more northerly
context? Alt has argued that Joshua is really only at home in
the incidents described in chs. 10 and 11, but even here much
of the activity purports to take place well outside an
Ephraimite milieu.

A close examination of chs. 1-12 shows that Joshua himself
sits very light to much of the material, and it is possible that
at some stage in the compilation of these traditions the figure
of Joshua has been introduced into episodes in which he in
fact played no part. It may be that we should think of the
development of these traditions as a phenomenon similar to

the growth of the cycles of legends about such figures as King Arthur or Robin Hood. There was perhaps a historical figure about whom stories were told. In the course of time these stories were elaborated, and additional tales, perhaps originally about other people or newly composed, became attached to such hero-figures. Once it is accepted that, in the end, the principal interest in such stories is not a historical one, it becomes easier to envisage that this might have happened.

Those who believe that behind the stories in Joshua there lie genuine historical reminiscences have defended a substantial historical role for Joshua. If, for example, the Israelites *did* take the huge (for its time) city of Hazor, an accomplished military commander capable of other great victories is likely to have been involved. Other suggestions about Joshua include the possibility that he was a charismatic figure similar to those about whom stories have bee preserved in the book of Judges. It has also been argued that the presentation of Joshua is based on the figure of King Josiah, who proclaimed the law to the people and represented them in the renewal of the covenant; thus Joshua would represent a type or pattern of the Israelite king. There are certainly a number of kingly features in the presentation of Joshua.

It was noted above that Joshua is presented as Moses' assistant and then successor. Sometimes in the book of Joshua he seems to be presented almost as a second Moses. The following similarities are particularly striking. The crossing of the Jordan under Joshua's leadership is reminiscent of the crossing of the Reed Sea under Moses' leadership. The instruction of the angel to Joshua before the advance on Jericho, 'Remove the sandals from your feet, for the place where you stand is holy' (5.15) recalls the instruction to Moses at the burning bush (Exod. 3.5). Joshua inscribes the law on stones (8.32; cf. 24.26), as does Moses according to Exod. 34.27-28. If an editor is deliberately seeking to make Joshua appear as a second Moses, does this call into question the historicity of some of the episodes?

Later traditions have tended to expand somewhat the picture of Joshua. For example, 1 Maccabees reports that

'Joshua, because he fulfilled the command, became a judge in Israel' (1 Macc. 2.55). In Ben Sirach's 'Hymn to the Fathers' there is a description of Joshua and his exploits (Ecclus 46.1-8): he is described as 'the successor of Moses in the prophetic office' (v. 1). And in 2 Esd. 7.37 (*4 Ezra* 7.107), Joshua is included in a list of those who prayed for other people. Such traditions do not really add anything to our knowledge of Joshua other than to make it clear that he continued to be revered as a great figure from the past.

The attempt to find extrabiblical evidence for Joshua's existence in one of the Tell el-Amarna letters, where a certain Yashuya is mentioned, cannot be sustained. Not only is it highly doubtful that the names can be equated, but the Amarna letters date from the fourteenth century BCE, i.e. before the date for the exodus of the Israelites from Egypt most widely accepted by those who regard it as historical.

Was there a Joshua? Certainty on this issue is impossible, but there may perhaps have been a man called Joshua who was a leader of the Ephraimites. To him have been attached a number of other traditions, notably from the tribe of Benjamin and Gilgal in particular. He is presented as one who was obedient to the will of Yahweh and who, as a consequence, was able to lead the people to the possession of the land with the help of the God who had promised it to them.

Further Reading

On the occupation and settlement:

A. Alt, 'The Settlement of the Israelites in Palestine', in *Essays on Old Testament History and Religion*, pp. 133-69.

Bright, *A History of Israel*.

Coote and Whitelam, *The Emergence of Early Israel in Historical Perspective*.

C.H.J. de Geus, *The Tribes of Israel* (Studia Semitica Neerlandica, 18; Assen: Van Gorcum, 1976).

D.N. Freedman and D.F. Graf (eds.), *Palestine in Transition: The Emergence of Ancient Israel* (The Social World of Biblical Antiquity, 2; Sheffield: Almond Press, 1983).

N.K. Gottwald, *The Tribes of Yahweh* (Maryknoll, NY: Orbis Books, 1979; London: SCM Press, 1980).

B. Halpern, *The Emergence of Israel in Canaan* (SBLMS, 29; Chico, CA: Scholars Press, 1983).

Lemche, *Ancient Israel*.

G.E. Mendenhall, 'The Hebrew Conquest of Palestine', *BA* 25 (1962), pp. 66-87.

—'Ancient Israel's Hyphenated History', in Freedman and Graf (eds.), *Palestine in Transition: The Emergence of Ancient Israel*, pp. 91-103.

J.M. Miller, 'The Israelite Occupation of Canaan', in J.H. Hayes and J.M. Miller (eds.), *Israelite and Judean History* (OTL; London: SCM Press, 1977), pp. 213-84.

M. Noth, *The History of Israel* (London: A. & C. Black, 2nd edn, 1960).

M. Weippert, *The Settlement of the Israelite Tribes in Palestine* (SBT 2nd series, 21; London: SCM Press, 1971).

On covenant:

Nicholson, *God and his People*.

L. Perlitt, *Bundestheologie im Alten Testament* (WMANT, 36; Neukirchen–Vluyn: Neukirchener Verlag, 1969).

On aetiology:

J. Bright, *Early Israel in Recent History Writing* (SBT, 19; London: SCM Press, 1956).

B.S. Childs, 'A Study of the Formula "Until this Day"', *JBL* 82 (1963), pp. 279-92.

—'The Etiological Tale Re-examined', *VT* 24 (1974), pp. 387-97.

A.H.W. Curtis, 'Aetiology', in R.J. Coggins and J.L. Houlden (eds.), *A Dictionary of Biblical Interpretation* (London: SCM Press; Philadelphia: Trinity Press International, 1990), pp. 8-10.

B.O. Long, *The Problems of Etiological Narrative in the Old Testament* (BZAW, 108; Berlin: Töpelmann, 1968).

8

THE BOOK OF JOSHUA: HISTORY, GEOGRAPHY, THEOLOGY?

The book of Joshua clearly sets out to present an account of events which purport to have happened in the past. As such, its purpose might be said to be 'historical'. Yet equally clearly, the inevitable conclusion arrived at in the light of the considerations of the preceding chapters is that much of the material in the book is not 'history' in the usually accepted sense of the term, even when it is accepted that there is no such thing as a completely objective and 'scientific' history.

This is not to say that there are no recollections of ancient events and no genuinely ancient materials preserved within the book. It has been noted, for example, that very early traditions from Gilgal and the area of Benjamin may well underlie some of the stories in the first half of the book. But traditions which may be based on actual events have undergone such a complicated process of transmission and adaptation that it is difficult, if not impossible, to discern the precise nature of the underlying happenings. Again, it is possible that real events lie somewhere in the background of traditions which, in the form in which they are presented in the book of Joshua, seem to have an aetiological interest or to have been shaped by cultic considerations. It is difficult to differentiate these from traditions which had aetiological or cultic origins. Some of the lists in the second half of the book may be ancient, but it is unlikely that any of them come from the period they purport to reflect.

The book of Joshua is therefore of very limited value for the task of reconstructing the story of what actually happened prior to the establishment of the monarchy in Israel. The result of its attempt to present a picture of a unified conquest under the leadership of a single military commander, and to do so by taking a handful of traditions which derived principally from a single rather small area and turning them into an account of the conquest of the whole land, can scarcely be termed history in that sense.

If the traditions in Joshua are not to be regarded as primarily historical, how are they to be understood? It is clear that in the latter half of the book there is a geographical interest, and it has been suggested that this interest is also dominant in the earlier chapters. The 'conquest' stories tell how the whole of the land came to belong to Israel. They do not present objective history but justify Israel's claim to all the territory up to the extent of the Davidic borders. Thus the 'conquest' traditions provide the context for the subsequent chapters which describe the allocation of the land among the various subdivisions of Israel—a land won for them thanks to the intervention of their God. It is noteworthy that the allotment of the land includes territory which may never really have been part of Israel, or which was only so much later, so the picture is ideal rather than real.

But is this interest really primarily geographical? The land is won not so much with the help of God as thanks to the activity of God. The presentation of some episodes of the 'conquest' in almost cultic terms and in terms which stress Yahweh's active participation in events (involving what has come to be known as the concept of 'Holy War'—see below) hints that the real interest goes beyond the historical or geographical, and is in fact theological. The book of Joshua begins with a recollection of God's promise. The story of the spies in ch. 2 paves the way for the fulfilment of the promise. The crossing of the Jordan is presented in terms reminiscent of a religious procession bearing the Ark (chs. 3–4). The central event, the capture of Jericho, is prepared for by circumcision (5.2-7), the keeping of the Passover (5.10-12—a passage which also mentions that God's provision of food for the people in the form of manna ceased at that point since new provision was made in the form of the fruits of the land) and the appearance of an angel (5.13-15). The actual conquest of Jericho is achieved with minimal human contribution other than to perform certain almost ritualistic actions (6.1-21). The devotion to destruction of Jericho and its subsequent breach by Achan (7.1-26) introduces a motif associated with Holy War. The act of disobedience has to be set right before the conquest of Ai can be achieved (8.1-29).

Is it possible that warfare in ancient Israel was actually brought into the cultic arena? That the biblical writers present Yahweh as a participant in war is clear. Such wars are referred to as 'wars of Yahweh', because of the stress on Yahweh's activity. Indeed, there is an intriguing hint in Num. 21.14 that there existed a 'book of the Wars of Yahweh'; although this is not cited as a source for any of the material in the book of Joshua. The phrase 'wars (or battles) of Yahweh's is also used in connection with the activities of David (1 Sam. 18.17; 25.28). It is also clear that a number of features recur in the various accounts of the wars of Yahweh, such as (1) the so-called 'handing-over formula' ('I have/the LORD has given...to you/into your hand'), (2) stress on the participation of Yahweh, perhaps in a miraculous or supernatural way, though sometimes by the empowering of human leaders, and (3) emphasis on the complete destruction of the enemy. These elements can be seen, for example, in the episode recounted in Josh. 10.6-11, and in the story of the fall of Jericho which contains the handing-over formula (6.16), the placing of the sacred ban on the city (6.17) and the miraculous collapse of the walls (6.20). It should, however, be stressed that there is no clear single pattern for the presentation of such stories despite the frequent recurrence of certain elements.

The formulaic presentation of such accounts led to the belief that there was in ancient Israel a concept of 'Holy War'. But does this reflect an actual practice, or is it simply the result of redactional activity? Von Rad stressed the cultic character of Holy War, and related it specifically to the period between the settlement and the establishment of the monarchy; but these historical limits have been felt by others to be too narrow. Von Rad believed that the stylized nature of the biblical presentation reflected something which *was* actually practised in the cult in ancient Israel. Smend, on the other hand, has taken the opposite view on both issues, that is, whether Holy War was ever practised and whether it was cultic. Jones has suggested that a 'Holy War schema' may have been founded on earlier traditions of the wars of Yahweh which were essentially non-cultic (although the ancient battles may have had 'cultic preliminaries'). The Holy War schema, by adopting patterns of formulae and cultic expressions, gave Yahweh's activity even greater prominence. Jones has also wondered whether it is possible that, at some later stage, the theory of Holy War actually influenced the practice. This would, of course, imply that the schema had been formulated in time to influence later practice. Jones cites as possibilities for such influence the Aramean wars recounted in 1 Kings 20 and the later Maccabean battles; the latter would allow for a late formulation of the schema, but the former would imply a relatively early (certainly pre-Deuteronomistic) date.

The possibility that earlier traditions about wars or battles which were used by the Deuteronomists already contained some elements which formed the basis of a Holy War schema cannot be ruled out. But it is impossible to say with certainty whether they adopted the schema because it fitted their ideas, or produced it in order to put over their ideas. In view of the Deuteronomists' liking for stereotyped formulae and stylized presentation the latter may seem more likely. That the Deuteronomists would wish to stress the active participation of Yahweh in events, notably in the giving of the land to Israel, cannot be doubted.

The main underlying claim made by the book of Joshua is that Yahweh has fulfilled his promises to the forefathers by giving them a land in which to dwell. To this extent the book of Joshua provides the context for the subsequent story of Israel in the land, as recorded in the remainder of the Deuteronomistic History. The giving of the law, the establishing of the covenant and the fulfilling of the promise of

land form the background against which the story of the
people's unfaithfulness and disobedience is told.

So in a work which sets out the acts of God in the story of
the chosen people, the book of Joshua has a significant part to
play. The earlier traditions which underlie some parts of the
book of Joshua doubtless originally had their own purposes
and their own ideas to convey, but these have been almost
entirely hidden by the overarching message which the
Deuteronomists use the traditions to present. And it is not
only the stories describing the conquest of the land as a result
of divine intervention which are important in teaching their
lesson. The fact that the distribution of the land is given in
such great detail is highly significant. *All* the land is involved,
and *all* the people are involved. The divine gift of the land is
for all, and all can share in God's blessing. It is also possible
that the lists enshrine what was thought to be a divinely
ordained structure for Israel's life within the Promised Land.

But it is above all in the 'conquest' stories that the hand of
God can be seen at work. The book of Joshua implies that the
conquest was successful because Joshua was faithful and
obedient, a true successor of Moses, and because the people
were faithful and obedient—apart from Achan, and stress is
laid on how he was punished. The result of faithfulness and
obedience was that God performed his act of grace on behalf
of his people.

It is clear what message the Deuteronomists sought to
convey to the people of a generation which had suffered the
loss of its land to the Babylonians and many of whom had
been forcibly removed from the land and taken into exile. Just
as disobedience had brought about the loss of their land, so
obedience would bring the reward of the land restored. The
God who was powerful enough to reduce Jericho, Ai, Hazor
and other great enemy strongholds to heaps of ruins was, by
implication, powerful enough to overthrow the enemies of the
descendants of those who first settled in the God-given land.

It was not only the disobedience of the people which had
contributed to the loss of the land, but the inadequacy of
those who were supposed to provide leadership—the kings of
Israel and Judah. What was required was faithful and

obedient leadership of the type offered by Joshua, the successor of God's servant Moses. So it is perhaps not surprising that similarities have been seen between the presentation of Joshua and that of Josiah, the one king to receive real approbation from the Deuteronomists:

> Before him [i.e. Josiah] there was no king like him, who turned to the LORD with all his heart, with all his soul, and with all his might, according to all the law of Moses; nor did any like him arise after him (2 Kgs 23.25).

Butler has neatly summed up the key themes of the book as: the land, the leadership, the law, the Lord. Chapters 1 and 23–24 have been described as 'brackets' to the book which underline its major theological emphases. God's words at the beginning of the opening chapter stress that the gift of the land rests on his promise. It is on the basis of that promise that the people are told to prepare for action. Joshua is urged to remain obedient, and the people in their turn pledge obedience to Joshua. The book ends with further calls to obedience and recollections of how God has kept his promise in what he has done for the people. In the farewell address in ch. 23 Joshua urges continued obedience: 'Therefore be very steadfast to observe and do all that is written in the book of the law of Moses, turning aside from it neither to the right nor to the left' (v. 6). Subsequently he reminds them that God has fulfilled his promises:

> And now I am about to go the way of all the earth, and you know in your hearts and souls, all of you, that not one thing has failed of all the good things that the LORD your God promised concerning you; all have come to pass for you, not one of them has failed (v. 14).

In the final chapter of the book, Joshua is presented as telling the people all that God achieved on their behalf, then confronting them with a choice:

> Now therefore revere the LORD and serve him in sincerity and in faithfulness; put away the gods that your ancestors served beyond the River and in Egypt, and serve the LORD. Now if you are unwilling to serve the LORD, choose this day whom you will serve, whether the gods your ancestors served in the region beyond the River or the gods of the Amorites in whose land you

are living; but as for me and my household, we will serve the
LORD (24.14-15).

Through the mouth of Joshua, the Deuteronomists put the
same choice *mutatis mutandis* to the people of their own day:
faithful obedience to Yahweh or the worship of other gods?
The stories which precede help the people to make up their
mind in favour of the God whose power they demonstrate.

It was noted earlier that, near the beginning of the book,
the question is asked, 'What do these stones mean?' (4.6, 21).
Here the question refers specifically to stones set up to mark
the crossing of the Jordan. But perhaps it is not inappropriate
to ask the question in more general terms about all the
'stones' of the book of Joshua—ruin stones, standing stones,
hailstones, boundary stones. The stones mean that Yahweh is
a powerful God who keeps his promises to those who are
faithful to him. The implication is that those who are disobedient will be punished, but those who are faithful will be
rewarded with God's blessing. This message is reminiscent of
prophetic calls to repentance and faithful obedience; the book
of Joshua is, after all, included among the Former Prophets in
the Hebrew canon of scripture.

Further Reading

G.H. Jones, 'The Concept of Holy War', in Clements (ed.), *The World of
    Ancient Israel*, pp. 299-321.
G. von Rad, *Der Heiliger Krieg im alten Israel* (ATANT, 20; Zurich:
    Zwingli-Verlag, 1951).
R. Smend, *Yahweh War and Tribal Confederation* (Nashville: Abingdon
    Press, 1970).

9
JOSHUA AS LITERATURE

A relatively recent trend in the study of the Old Testament
has seen an emphasis on the literary appreciation of the final
form of the text of a section of a book, a whole book, or even a
group of books. This approach has contrasted with other
critical methods, in particular form-criticism with its emphasis
on isolating and analysing individual units of tradition. This
type of literary appreciation has begun to make an impact on
the study of the book of Joshua.

B.S. Childs, who pioneered an approach which has come to
be known as 'canonical criticism' (although Childs has
indicated his unhappiness with the term), stresses the tension
between fulfilment and non-fulfilment in the book of Joshua.
This theme is present in the depiction of the conquest. On the
one hand it is presented as a complete conquest of the whole
land, but on the other hand there are passages (cf. also Judg.
1) which suggest that the action was not united but piecemeal
and that not all the Canaanites were driven out. Within the
description of the allocation of the land there is a tension
between passages which suggest a division of the whole of the
land among the tribes and passages which point to an
incomplete picture, with some groups who have yet to receive
their allotted territories. This tension was used by the editor in
a 'homiletical fashion' to encourage obedience.

D.M. Gunn, a staunch defender of the literary approach to
biblical material, has also drawn attention to the tension

between complete and incomplete fulfilment in the book of
Joshua, and has suggested that the recognition of this overarching tension allows other tensions to be seen. The sparing
of Rahab was, in effect, a breach of the 'ban' placed on those
who fell into the hands of the Israelites; what happened as a
result of the sparing of Rahab contrasts starkly with the fate
of Achan who broke the 'ban'. This raises questions such as
whether the gift of the land is truly unconditional or
dependent on complete obedience, and whether the law must
be adhered to strictly (as with Achan) or whether there may
be some scope for modification (as with those who spared
Rahab). The land *is* a gift, but obedience *is* required; this is
the tension between divine justice and divine mercy.

Gunn's survey is clearly indebted to R.M. Polzin's literary
study of the Deuteronomistic History. Polzin has sought to
differentiate between *reported* speech (for example of God or
of Moses) and *reporting* speech (of the narrator). He notes
that within the book of Joshua it is the latter that
predominates. The book of Joshua is described as 'a sustained
meditation on what it means to interpret the word of God in
general and the book of the law in particular'. The description
of the occupation of the land enables the narrator to give an
account of Israel's application of the law. The distance
between the commands of the law and Joshua's (hence
Israel's) fulfilment of them is seen by Polzin as the underlying
theme of chs. 1–12. The distance between God's promises
about the land and his fulfilment of them is the theme of chs.
13–21. The distance between the divine word and the human
interpretation is the theme of chs. 22–24 and is the general
theme of the whole book. Also at issue is Israel's own identity
as, Polzin suggests, both citizen and alien. Those who are
'exceptional outsiders' function in the story as *types* of Israel,
and the book of Joshua shows how much that is 'outside' both
communally and territorially is in fact 'inside'. The audiences
addressed by the Deuteronomistic narrator were probably
located outside the land of Israel and could therefore take
comfort from the fact that they had in a sense always been
outsiders even when in the land.

Polzin also suggests that some of the summary statements, which are found at key places in the book of Joshua and which appear to claim total success for the Israelites, must be understood as ironic. The author, he claims, allows this 'voice of authoritarian dogmatism' to be heard, even on the lips of such authoritative characters as Joshua, despite the fact that the narrative has made it clear that such statements are not to be taken literally. This suggestion has been taken up positively and elaborated by L. Eslinger in his narratological approach to the Deuteronomistic History. He points out that the function of irony is to expose the weakness of the viewpoint it purports to express. In Joshua there is a quite deliberate exposure of the claims of complete success on the part of the Israelites as not matching the reality of what is actually narrated. Read thus, the book of Joshua ceases to be full of inconsistency and incoherence and does not, for example, contradict the picture given in Judges 1. The role of the narrator is thereby seen to be authoritative.

L.D. Hawk's study of the book of Joshua concentrates on matters of plot as a key to understanding its message. Plot can be understood on a number of levels: at its most basic it may refer to a story's general framework, but it can also be understood in terms of the arrangement and relationship of incidents one to another, or may even place stress on the mind that does the organizing of incidents rather than on the incidents themselves. Hawk's study notes patterns of coherence and dissonance within the book, and this leads him to stress the theme of 'desire': Israel's desire is for land, whereas Yahweh's desire is for Israel's allegiance and, in particular, for the type of communion enshrined in the idea of covenant. Ironically it is the land that threatens Yahweh's desire. Both Israel and Yahweh desire an end that is unfulfilled. The narrator's desire is to present a picture of an obedient Israel in unrivalled possession of the land. This too remains unfulfilled, as examples of victory and obedience are countered by instances of infidelity and lack of success, and the narrator finds it increasingly difficult to sustain his desire to assert the fidelity and integrity of Israel as the story progresses, although he continues to do so. Attention is also drawn by

Hawk to the reader's desire to cope with the tension between dogma and experience which may mirror the tension inherent in Israel's claims to a fulfilment which was unfulfilled.

L. Rowlett's reading of the book of Joshua notes that the apparent sharp distinction between 'Israel' and 'others' soon begins to break down. Rahab, an 'outsider', became an 'insider'; Achan, an 'insider', became an 'outsider'. It is suggested that the book is about the assertion of power and the maintenance of authority. Violent action in pursuit of these ends is justified. By submitting to Joshua's authority Rahab became an 'insider', but the book also warns potential Achans on the inside that failure to obey authority can result in their becoming outsiders. Rowlett contends that this key to understanding the book reflects the time of Josiah's attempt to consolidate his kingdom when monarchical authority was far from secure.

Literary approaches have brought fresh insights to bear on the study of the biblical material. They also raise a number of questions. To what extent do they engage in exegesis and to what extent do they indulge in eisegesis? Are they seeking to discover the original purpose of the writer or redactor, or to analyse what a later reader may discern in the text or how that reader may respond to the text? To what extent was it the concern of the book to produce a rounded literary piece, or to preserve a variety of traditions about Israel's sacred past? There can be no doubt that there is a tension between fulfilment and non-fulfilment in the book of Joshua, but is this a conscious literary ploy or the result of a real tension between history and theology? There may be theological implications in the acceptance of some of the suggestions noted above. If the book of Joshua is really about obedience to monarchical authority, this must to some extent challenge the view that it is about obedience to divine authority. If the claims for complete success in the occupation are ironic, then their theological significance as assertions that, despite what appears to be evidence to the contrary, God *is* in control and *does* fulfil his promises appears to be diminished. In a book in which God is in fact the leading protagonist it would be surprising if the primary interest were not theological.

Further Reading

B.S. Childs, *Introduction to the Old Testament as Scripture* (London: SCM Press, 1979).

L. Eslinger, *Into the Hands of the Living God* (JSOTSup, 84; Sheffield: JSOT Press, 1989).

D.M. Gunn, 'Joshua and Judges', in R. Alter and F. Kermode (eds.), *The Literary Guide to the Bible* (London: Collins, 1987).

—'New Directions in the Study of Hebrew Narrative', *JSOT* 39 (1987), pp. 65-75.

L.D. Hawk, *Every Promise Fulfilled: Contesting Plot in Joshua* (Literary Currents in Biblical Interpretation; Louisville, KY: Westminster Press/John Knox, 1991).

R.M. Polzin, *Moses and the Deuteronomist: A Literary Study of the Deuteronomic History* (New York: Seabury, 1980).

L. Rowlett, 'Inclusion, Exclusion and Marginality in the Book of Joshua', *JSOT* 55 (1992), pp. 15-23.

See also G. Mitchell, *Together in the Land: A Reading of the Book of Joshua* (JSOTSup, 134; Sheffield: JSOT Press, 1993).

INDEXES

INDEX OF REFERENCES

INDEX OF NAMES

DATE DUE

CPSIA information can be obtained at www.ICGtesting.com
Printed in the USA
LVOW08s2126060914

402827LV00019B/907/P